I
Know Why
Mandingos
Sing

The Real Reason Why
African Americans Are So
Deadly To Each Other

Donald E. Payne
Sacramento, California

This Book is dedicated to The Memory of Anna
Louise Marshall Ridgeway and Henry Elroy Ridgeway Sr.

Published by   RCMG-Publishing
Copyright © 2011   RCMG-Publishing
Cover Copyright © 2011   RCMG-Publishing

Title ID: 3692969
ISBN-13: 978-1466355866

10 9 8 7 6 5 4 3 2 1
First Edition first printing: October 2011

Printed in the United States Of America

Contents

Preface - **6**

Introduction - **9**

Chapter I - The Abduction - **20**

The Mandinka People - **25**

Shaka Zulu - **28**

Chapter II - Portrait The African Mandinka Male - **31**

Chapter III - Portrait The African Mandinka Female - **36**

Chapter IV – Portrait The American Mandinka Man - **39**

The proud black man - **43**

Joe Louis - **44**

Sugar Ray Robinson - **44**

Jack Johnson - **45**

Wilma Rudolf - **46**

Jesse Owens - **47**

Black Music - **47**

Blackman in the 60s - **48**

The Angry Black Man - **49**

Black Crime - **52**

Black On Black Crime - **53**

Police Brutality - **55**

Chapter V - Portrait Of The American Mandinka Woman - **58**

Angry Black Women - **63**

Chapter VI - Portrait Of The White Anglo Sachsen Male - **69**

White Male Brutality - **72**

Carl Peters - **75**

White crime - **79**

Chapter VII - Portrait Of The White Anglo Sachsen Woman - **85**

White Female Brutality - **88**

Chapter VIII - American Mandinka Men-Anglo Sachsen Women - **91**

Status symbol - **96**

Chapter IX - American Mandinka Women-Anglo Sachsen Man - **103**

Chapter X - Black Entertainment - **110**

Chapter XI - The Media - **103**

Religion and the Media- **115**

The Internet - **120**

Chapter XII Conclusion – **124**

Black mothers - **128**
Black daughters - **133**
Black fathers - **136**
Black sons - **139**
Black Achievements - **145**

Preface

I know why Mandingos sing represents years of research, study, gathering material, information and interviews by the author and is presented as a documented account of and comparison to the psyche of the West African and the African American Mandinka people. Provocative-historical account of the Mandinka (Mandingo) secrets and attitudes that have kept them down since the 13th century. This book is not for everyone, there is a special audience that I am trying to reach in this account. And this book is not about African Americans or Africans singing, it's about the un-justice that has been bestowed upon us by Jewish and White slave merchants with the help of our brothers, side by side to aid THEM in their rampage to capture and destroy the African (American) Mandinka people. But mostly this book is about our mental psychological and physical attitudes that makes us so venomous against each other.

But I am also writing this book for another audience as well and that is the friends, relatives, neighbours, community, teachers, co-workers and especially Black politicians who seem to not be able to get off of their butts. For those who do not "appreciate" the magnitude of our dilemma and the brutality that we have faced and are still facing and having survived, this is for you... I am writing this book for all of those trapped in American society and trying to get out of the vicious and cruel cycle in America; and for those who have struggled and are still struggling to get ahead in life. And of course for all of the 100,000,000 brothers and sisters that did not survive the North Atlantic Slave Trade and it's inhumane brutality and sustainability. To research and study the origin of our hatred for each other and compare our acts during the 13th century with our present day perception of what it is that makes us tick the way we do. This book is especially written for those Mandingos in our society who are living in denial and who have lost their way, think that you have nothing to offer society, and don't know who they are...

I Know Why Mandingos Sing
Thoughts On Being Black In America

Introduction

Up until Today, Black people in America have not been able to shake the atrocities that the diabolical and un-human Jewish and White masters of slavery did to us. Many of the problems that African American Mandinka have with each other today are direct results of enslavement, our "Mental Capacity" and the techniques that they used to keep us in bondage. This mixed with the natural state of the Mandinka people which was submissiveness, betrayal, jealousy and hatred for our brothers, has manifested itself into Black urban warfare in the Unites States of America. Today approximately 40 million Mandinka people live in America and are the direct descendents of a race of people that were taken from their home lands in West Africa that need help-I will try with examples to show how we as African Americans are no different than our brothers and sisters living in West Africa and connect these behavior patterns to that type of behavior which we are seeing in America among Black people on a daily basis.

Betrayal, envy, hatred and distrust have always been inherited traits of Mandinka people; we are tenacious like crabs in our ways and still hold on to many antiquated African beliefs and myths, and today have little respect for each other because betrayal and self betrayal have plagued us for hundreds of years. And the first betrayals started as early as the end of the 13th century when Arabians with the help of their African counterparts, started kidnapping West Africans and taking them from their homes and land in West Africa for the slave market. But without the help of other Mandinka tribes, Arabians, Europeans nor Jews could not have taken any slaves. The Mandinka People were scattered and shipped all over North, and South America and The West Indies. And by them doing this it set the stage for this little nappy head Mandingo boy to enter the world of the White Anglo Saxon Arian male.

...

9

I was born on December 17, 1947 in Mobile Alabama as a Mandinka child. My parents loved each other, but my dad unfortunately had to leave us at an early age, even though most of the 11 children that they conceived together were adults. My parents were very smart and they were both honour students in high school. My childhood was very exciting and basically uncomplicated, even though we did have problems with the neighbourhood White males. But I enjoyed every minute of it. One thing that my dad taught me before he died was the importance of family and to keep your word. My dad was not the type that would whip his children, and when he did it was only a few licks and only when you did not do what he told you to, or when my mother told him to. And the guys in the family could basically do what they wanted to-but he would always explicitly say to us "If you get put in jail-don't call me". I guess his theory was, you had no business being there in the first place. Psychology is a b...h ain't it? I think that this statement helped us stay out of trouble. But one thing that would definitely get you knocked out was to fight one of your siblings. For my father this was a complete no-no. He never whipped or chastised the girls, but my mother would tear your AZ up. And as far as I can remember my dad never ever had a vocal or physical confrontation with my mother.

My mother was a very strong, religious and loving Mandinka African American woman who's singing talents could match that of any singer that ever stood on a stage. But she only sang for the Lord-and she taught me and other siblings in the family how to play the piano. My mother, as all the other moms in the neighbourhood raised the children and took care of the household. Dad had a job as a welder on the docks in Mobile and provided for the family as good as he could, because as you know at that time "niggers" hardly had jobs. Anyway I was a little bit better than an average student in school, but I really didn't try very hard either. I thought that I knew everything, boy was I wrong... I finally graduated from high school, went to college got drafted into the military, got out, and went back to Europe. Since then I have travelled the world and gathered much knowledge through experiences with peoples from all walks of life. This coupled with my awareness of the African and African American mindset, and my personal commitment and probing to get to the bottom of the conflicts between African Americans and find out what the problem really is, set the stage for my current beliefs pertaining to the relationship between the "modern" Mandinka man and woman living in America today.

By me being out side of the realm so to say, and looking in, I can see many things about the behaviour of our people in America that correlates with the West African mindset and cultural behaviour patterns that probably many Black male or female Americans are unaware of. Because of this I would like give my account as to what I think is happening with the African American Mandinka people. But in order to do this we will have to go back into history and time in order to see what I think at least 60% of the problem is. I must tell you here that I am not a historian or author, but I have an education, and am a man of the world, not to mention that I am a Black man which gives me the right to write these words, even though it took a long time for me to get to the point to say these things. I think that we as African Americans must learn to look at our ancestry for what it really is. So let's go back a few hundred years and look at what happen before and during the slave trade in order to try and get some type of understanding and piece this puzzle together.

First, let's look at where we come from-Africa-centre of the world, middle point, the cradle of civilization; and this is where OUR story began many, many, many years ago and up to now, "Civilization" has not changed US one bit.

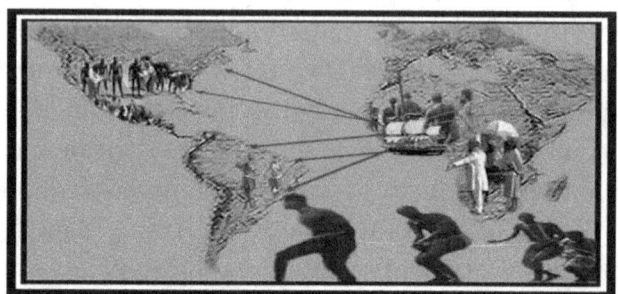

Jewish Slave Ship Routes

But isn't it ironic that what first started out as a religious crusade ended up in the enslavement of a continent and 100,000,000 of its inhabitants? Slavery was not an institution that was invented in the Middle Ages. In ancient times it was that the loosing side in a war between two Peoples were enslaved and made to pay for their misfortune with servitude. But nothing in human history, will ever compare to the North Atlantic slave trade (perpetrated by Jewish slave merchants, 1441-1840) in its magnitude, cruelty, brutality and demonic sustainability-not even the "**Holocaust**".

The cruel and inhuman Atlantic slave trade was a combination of religious, political and social developments in Western Europe and North Africa. There is much literature on this subject and it has been extensively analyzed by both the European and African perspectives. The Carnegie Institute of Technology in America also provides extensive reports and documents on the North Atlantic slave trade, especially the "Jewish" involvement. Through the examination of Muslim history one can see how the slave trade was at first influenced by events in North Africa and how it influenced Muslim societies in West Africa. In the final stage, slavery reached its peak, robbing Africa of millions of men, women and children. And it is believed that the first people to be targeted for slavery in West Africa were the Moors; at that time the Moors were Africans that the Portuguese and the Spanish referred to regardless of racial differences. History tells us that through the writings of Azurara, a Portuguese writer whose writings in 1441 revealed that a certain young Portuguese captain named Golcalves Tristao sailed along the coast of southern Morocco and Mauritania gathering ivory and other goods for sale in Lisbon. By chance he met an African couple (Moors), wounded the man with a javelin (spear) and took them both aboard his ship as slaves. The couple was presented to Prince Henry who was at that time governor of the Portuguese colony called Tangier (North Africa). Sensing an opportunity to capture more slaves, he authorized a raid the same year led by captain Tristao who was familiar with the Atlantic coast line of West Africa.

Captain Tristao and his crew captured more than a dozen Africans and enslaved them. And in 1444 the Portuguese Lagos Company chartered under the patronage of Prince Henry started to process slaves like cattle. At first, the capture of a few slaves did not cause a stir in Lisbon because there were already many African and Muslim slaves in Portugal and Spain. But when the richer merchants in Lisbon realized the benefits of owning slaves, and with the blessings and condolences of the Pope, investment in the slave trade increased, and in 1443 an expedition was organized and financed explicitly to capture more African slaves. Now don't forget that many Mandinka had already changed their indigenous beliefs to Islam during the 13th century. The shippers were, the Portuguese, the British, the French, the Spanish, the Dutch, and American Jewish merchants. The Germans on the other hand did other terrible and horrible things in "Deutsch Ost Africa". The slave traders had outposts on different African coasts where they purchased humans from African slave traders which is currently estimates at around 100,000,000 people, but we all know that the actual number of people taken from their homes in Africa is higher because untold numbers died from the long treks and at sea. The sick were cast overboard, men were beaten and women abused. During the 19th century, when the British navy imposed a search and impound policy towards slave ships, entire "human cargo" were thrown overboard to prevent the ships from being impounded. Many more millions were killed in the tribal wars that were fought in Africa to capture the Mandinka people. When all these numbers are added up, a conservative, figure for the total casualties of the brutal North Atlantic slave trade would probably be more than 110,000,000 Africans. And to bring these numbers into perspective, the total population of England around the year 1600 was estimated at six million people. Almost all of the slave captives were from West Africa, a region that was under Islamic influence for decades. One can assume that up to 80-90% of all African slaves that were transported to the Americas were Mandinka people who were captured by their Mandinka Muslim brothers, and Africa was denied the energy of its young men and young women. Instead, they became a commodity item to be sold that helped Jews and Whites accumulate enormous capital in Europe and the Americas.

Jewish Merchants have a 2000 year old history in the involvement with slavery; this includes Black, Indian and White salves, and one of the first to feel the savagery and brutality of Jewish merchants were the American Indians. One can find all kinds of information about the story of slavery in America which actually began with Christopher Columbus who's voyage to America was financed by Luis De Santangelo which began August 3, 1492. He was accompanies by five "Marcanos" who were Jewish merchants who had denounced their religion and supposedly became Catholics; they convinced Columbus to capture 500 native American Indians to be sold in Seville Spain as slaves-after this horrible deed was carried out, Columbus of course did not receive any money for the sale of the slaves, but instead became the victim of a conspiracy conjured up by the 5 Marconas Jews and suffered as his reward injustice and

14

imprisonment through the betrayal of the Jews that he had trusted and helped; and this ironically was the beginning of the slave trade in the Americas.

The Jews were expelled from Spain in 1492 and from Portugal in 1497 for their dubious conduct, and many migrated to Holland where they setup the Dutch West Indies Company to exploit the New World. The Portuguese Jews that fled to the Netherlands where welcomed for their business skills. They began in the early 1500s to establish themselves in the Dutch and English colonies in the new world-they included Surinam, Curacao, Recife, New Amsterdam, Barbados, Newport, and Jamaica. Both North American and Caribbean Jews played a key roll in the commerce of slave trade.

1707 slave trade and sales records reveal that the Dutch West Indies company made the 10 largest purchases of slaves by Jewish merchants which comprised more than 25% of the total slaves sold. Jacob Barsimson was one of the first Jewish merchants who immigrated in 1664 from Holland to New Amsterdam which was New York at the time, and within the next decade many more Jews would follow.

Even then they were subjected by laws preventing them from engaging in the domestic economy, they quickly realized that all the territory owned by the native American Indians would be free and fertile field for them to do their dirty work because there were no laws preventing them form trading with the Indians. And the first Jewish merchant to start trading with the Indians was Heyman Levy who imported cheap textiles, glass beads earrings etc. from Holland and traded then for expensive furs (and that is why the settlers and trappers almost decimated the wild animal population in America). Levi was soon joined by Nicholas Lowe and Joseph Simon-Lowe conceived the idea of selling and trading rum and whisky to the Indians, and within a short period of time, set up 22 distilleries in Newport (all owned by Jews) to produce these liquors.

Newport became the center of commerce for the dealings in rum, whisky and liquor, and it finally became the center of the dealing of slaves. And it was from this port that the ships left for Africa to gather their Black human cargo, and amass great sums of money in exchange for them. According to Authentic reports, out of 128 ships that unloaded their human cargo in Charleston within a years time, 120 of them were owned and undersigned with their own names by Jewish merchants from Newport and Charleston. Even ships entering Boston, Norfolk and Baltimore, the real owners were the Jewish dealers from Newport and Charleston.

Because of the 1661 prohibition against slavery all of the colonies had lost many of their slaves, but it was in that year that the Jews had become powerful enough to bring about an appeal of these laws, and this is when slavery began to thrive. Following the Revolutionary war, the Jewish merchants had already found a loophole that would give them total freedom, so they "schemed" to make slavery legal, and some of the people in Philadelphia that were requesting the existing laws pertaining to slavery be eliminated were Jews Santiford, Woolman, Solomon, Levi, and Venevet. The Jews were only concerned with their own freedom and civil rights which had been withheld from them by the American government. After the revolutionary war the Jews were given equal rights and freed of all restrictions. But the question is, what happen to the Mandinka people that were captive there? They remained slaves of course, and by 1750 1/6 of the population of New York were Mandinka.

In order to achieve their goals, which was the world wide distribution of African slaves, the Jewish influence had to help keep the slaves in slavery. But the Jew that probably played the most significant overall part in the slave trade was Aaron Lopez. Lopez and his family fled Portugal and came to America (Newport) around 1750. He came as a member of the Melano family with the Christian name of Don Durate Lopez, once in America he dropped his Christian name and took back his Hebrew name of Aaron. And within 20 years Lopez owned or had interest in over 80 sailing vessels; he was also one of the founder of the Touro Synagogue, and was known as one of the merchant princes of early America trading in rum, dry goods and African slaves.

Between 1726 and 1774 Lopez had more than 50% of all dealings under his personal control. Aaron Lopez is one name that all Mankinka people living in America should remember, he was a Jewish slave merchant who owned many slave ships. But Jewish people never get any press from this because they own and control the press themselves. There is much evidence about the Jewish involvement in the North Atlantic slave trade, but the part that they played is never mentioned. They are the ones who pushed the slave trade in North America. Even though White people are blamed for these atrocities committed against mankind, they were only partly involved, because very few Whites owned slave ships. So in reality it was Jewish merchants who kept the slave trade alive, and you never hear anything about their evil deeds. The Jewish involvement is so historical that someone should pay more attention to it.

But the Jews on the other hand rant and rave about the Holocaust, when in fact they are the ones responsible for the inhumane, savage treatment and death of over 100,000,000 African slaves. More than 15 times the number of Africans died at the hands of Jewish merchants as Jews died at the hands of the Germans, so what do they have to complain about? And even many Jewish historians allegedly brag about their domination of the slave trade since ancient times and many more zealous writers of Jewish history actually boast about the domination of the "Jewish Triangular Slave Trade" between Africa, the West Indies and the American colonies; but ironically Jewish people never get any "PRESS" from their actions because as I said,

Jewish people own and control the press, and even Sam Francis former editorial editor of the Washington Times lost his job for merely commenting on things about the Jewish supremacy, and quoted different Jewish historians bragging about the Jewish domination of the slave trade since ancient times. But the conspiracy of silence is very evident; even Rabbi Morris A. Gustein contended in his book "The Story Of The Jews In Newport" attempted to say that there is no evidence of the Jewish involvement in the North Atlantic Slave Trade; but the Carnegie Institute of Technology printed and made public authentic documents entitled "Documents Illustrative Of The History Of The Slave Trade In America" which contain numerous documented shipping letters, letters to the slave dealers, and letters to the ships captains which was about 50% Jewish as proof of to the Jewish involvement in the North Atlantic Slave Trade.

The true story about the African Mandinka slave is fully and truthfully documented and available for the world to see and read through the Carnegie Institute of Technology located in Pittsburgh Pennsylvania. The Jews have denied for centuries that they had anything to do with the enslavement of the Mankinka people of West Africa, but the Carnegie Institute of Technology shows you that this is "NOT TRUE, and thanks to the research of Dr. Walter White Jr. one can say with certainty that the Jewish influence and involvement in the slave trade is more than adequately documented, and documented by a very reputable establishment.

Neither books or newspapers were published on the subject of the brutal Jewish involvement in the slave trade and it's no wonder that most Americans and people of the world do not know about these terrible atrocities that the Jews committed against the negro, and the Jews that knew what was going on were of course keeping their mouths shut. The Jews always want people to believe that they are the innocent, abused and prosecuted people; this has always been their strategy to gain sympathy for their cause, but the thing is that Jews keep score, they have made a tradition out of prosecution. Just remember that Jewish people hands are "NOT" free of the blood of untold millions of Mandinkan people. They owned slave ships and they bought, sold, raped and robbed us.

So when the Jews were punished, beaten and murdered, they had to leave Spain and Portugal. Where did you go? They went to the Caribbean and South America where they became plantation owners to continue there, their sadistic "Hand Werk".

I'm not a hater, my passion is for truth and justice, but there is hardly any Jewish person brave enough to read their history that will come away saying that their hands are cleaned. And this is why Blacks in America cannot get their reparations because the Jewish lobby is preventing it and Jews will never tell the truth about what really happen during the brutal and sustained North Atlantic slave trade.

Chapter I
The Abduction

Arabian, European, Jewish and African slave traders with captured Mandinka in holding area.

In order to understand and comprehend the slave trade, we must look closer at the Jewish handwork which gave then influence and power. Because since that time there has been much written about the slave trade by many zealous Jewish writers devoted to the idea of slavery that has been clouded up for many generations in their attempt to hide the truth about the Jewish involvement in the salve trade. Jewish agencies were set up off the coast of Africa as an African agency only to buy, sell and deal in African slaves. These agencies reached deep into West Africa, and they captured Africans corralled them and prepared them for sale; and the method they used to win over the heads of villages and chiefs for the Jewish slave trade was similar to the method they employed with the American Indians. So the first thing that they would do was to present the chiefs with rum in exchange for gold and ivory, and they soon found themselves in a drunken delirium from the liquor, and when the gold and ivory supplies were exhausted, they were induced to sell their people, men women and children; and some tribes began warfare to capture other Mandinka tribes, all instigated by the Jews merchants. The captured prisoners were exchanged for rum, ammunition and guns for the capturers to use in their campaigns to capture more Mandinka people. As I mentioned before the shippers were, the Portuguese, the British the French, the Spanish, the Dutch, American and West Indian Jewish merchants. But the ones that had the most impact on and profit from the slave trade were the Portuguese Jews that had converted to Christianity, the Brazilian Jews and American Jews who had formed a triangle slave trade between Africa, North America and the Caribbean; but they also convinced Dutch, English and French Jews to help provide them with slaves for the colonies.

After the slaves were captured they had to be taken to the Atlantic coast for processing. The men were separated from the women, and the children usually stayed up on deck; the men were transported in a box like area with only a few inches between them. Their quarters were bad enough but the women's were truly despicable, all of the excrements, women giving birth while being pressed close together, being raped by the captain and crew resulting thereby in the first mulatto babies being born after they came to America. Because of the horrendous conditions, people of course went crazy and fights broke out especially among the men, which could only to be contained by the bull whip. Many of them died during the long treks from the interior of West Africa to the coast, and the only thing that would encourage them to move on was the bull whip. And according to reports, 9 out of 10 Africans died before they reached American soil. When you consider the yearly exodus of one Million Mandinkan slaves one can imagine the extensive exodus of Mandinka slaves taken out of West Africa. For every one million salves that made it to American soil nine million did not survive. They were driven together and were restrained with the help of other Mandinka and guard dogs, branded like you brand a horse to be identified with their Jewish owners which of course made them indeed the "Property" of Jewish merchants and they were held until they were to be shipped out of the docks. And if any of them tried to escape the sharp dogs would help retrieve them. After the recapture, they would take at least one of them and cut off his legs as a deterrent to the rest of them. The Jewish agents that always represented the chiefs dealt with the captain of the ship; one slave was valued at around 100 gallons of rum which was watered down as much as possible, or 100 pounds of gun powder or in cash 18-20 dollars; but the slaves were resold for up to 2000 dollars each. So you can see how deceitful they were, and what devilish tricks the Jews used to get their human slave cargo.

This is how Jewish merchants were able amass great amounts of money quickly by cheating their African slave captors, just as they did with Christopher Columbus. Of course some slaves managed through insurrection to gain control of one or the other ship, and one ship in particular, The 3 Friends tortured and tormented their Black human cargo so bad that they mutinied in a bloody rebellion, killed the captain, the crew, and turned the ship around back towards Africa; the Amistad was another, and ninety percent of the time most ships had non Jewish captains.

We were brutally kidnapped from our home, country and love ones. Basically the salve trade started in Senegal and most of the 100,000,000 slaves were transported from ports in this country. Senegal is located on the west coast of Africa-above Senegal are the western Sahara countries such as Mali which stretches down to the northern part of West Africa and Mauritanian. Further north are countries such as Morocco and Algeria. East of Algeria is Libya, and of course east of Libya is Egypt which lies on the

Mediterranean and the Red Sea, and is in the North East African Region. The Arabian Peninsula lies on the Red Sea, Gulf of Aden and the Arabian Sea. And if I'm not mistaken the institution of slavery was conceived by the Muslim people. This whole area from Senegal in West Africa across the entire northern part to the north eastern part of the continent was and still is controlled by the Muslims. Of course we all know, or maybe some of us don't know, that the slave trade was started at first by the Portuguese and then North Africans with the help of their Mandinka counterparts who had converted to Islam, and Tribes like the Fula participated in the capture. So what happen was that, some of the African countries which lie under the west Sahara regions fell victim to Arabian and Mandinka aggression, and were captured and enslaved by their (Muslim) Mandinka brothers who had already converted to Islam.

The population of Mali is entirely black, but predominately Muslims; and after Black Africans converted to Islam they started in an alcoholic "Rausch" to capture other Mandinka for the North Atlantic slave trade and to pay their Jewish slave traders for the watered down rum and gun powder which they had received. Many of them came from Senegal, Nigeria, Ghana, Liberia, Benin, and Sierra Leone. They preferred Nigerians because they had many "BIG BLACK BUCKS" to be used for breeding purposes. Sudan for instance is in east Africa, so the slaves from that side of the continent were sent to Saudi Arabia or Egypt to serve as slaves in harems or as sex slaves, which I might add that after children of sex slaves were born most of them were immediately killed. Most of the slaves were transported from Senegal to the new world, and if you look at the map you will see that North, Middle and South America are west of Africa. North of Africa is Europe. And out of the Europeans, the Portuguese at first were more active in the slave trade than most other countries, they transported many of the slaves to the new world, and if you check your map you will see that Portugal and Spain are only a few hundred miles from Africa, and by 1490, more than 3,000 slaves a year were transported to Portugal from Africa. But the Dutch eventually became the leaders because of the Dutch (Christian) Jews who were in "cahoots" with the American Jews. But during this time there was nothing unusual about the African slave trade until 1492, and the slave trade started to diminish towards the end of the 15th century; but by that time Lisbon had at least 10,000 African and Muslim slaves. Many of the slaves from sub-Saharan Africa were sold in North Africa, Spain and India. All supported by their African Mankinka brothers in crime. I think that the mentality that we inherited from our ancestors speak loud enough for our behaviour towards each other today. This is what I think the basic problem is. And if we don't recognize that, then we won't get better or heal as a race of people.

Jewish Slave Ship

So here we are in the new world-and even though we can't speak the language or communicate among ourselves, we still harbour this basic "Tribal" hatred for each other that we inherited form our forefathers which would manifest itself further down the road. This is something that is unprecedented in many other races. And the White man knew and took advantage of the inherent quality that we have to brutalize each other. This type demeanour helps me explain our situation a little bit better, we have it, we can't deny it, but we don't recognize it. This type of situation coupled with hatred, envy, frustration, death, or any type of situation which was and still is demeaning to us will eventually destroy us. And what do we do? Turn on each other. We still do the same things that our ancestors did during the 13th century and that is to wage war, kill and destroy each other. And that is why we as descendents of the Mandinka (Mandingo) people act the way we do towards each other today. I'm a firm believer that in order to understand your future you must know and understand your past. So let's take a closer look at our past... This brief history of the Mandinkan people will help me clarify this a bit more.

The Mandinka People

The **Mandingo language** (*Mandink'a*) is a Mandé language spoken by millions of Mandinka people in Mali, Senegal, The Gambia, Guinea, Côte d'Ivoire, Burkina Faso, Sierra Leone, Liberia, Guinea-Bissau and Chad; it is the main language of The Gambia, which belongs to the "Manding" branch of the Mandé language, and is thus fairly similar to Bambara and Monika or Malinké. And Black people, just for the record-African American women are not Nubian queens, they are Mandinka queens and princesses-I know that most all of us, me included, like to refer to the Black woman as my Nubian queen, and that's ok-but the truth of the matter is-Nubia is a region along the Nile, between Northern Sudan and Southern Egypt, no where near West Africa.

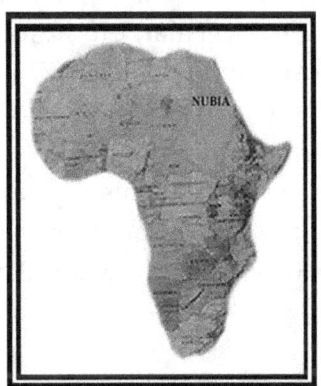

There were a number of small Nubian kingdoms throughout the middle ages, the last of which collapsed in 1504 when Nubia then became divided between Egypt and the Sennar Sultanate resulting in the Arabization of much of the Nubian population.

The *Mali Empir, Mandinka Empire* or *Manden Kurufa* was a West African empire of the Mandinka from c. 1230 to c. 1600. The empire was founded by Sundiata Keita and became renowned for the wealth of its rulers, especially Mansa Musa I. The Mali empire extended over a large area and consisted of numerous kingdoms and provinces. The Mandinka people are said to have migrated from west of the Niger River (which would be in Mali), into the heartlands of West Africa. Legend has it that they are the original inhabitants of the legendary ancient city of Djenné-Jeno. Originally from Mali, the Mandinka people gained their independence from previous empires in the thirteenth century, and founded an empire which stretched across West Africa. It is said that this great migration from their home lands west of the Niger River was in search of better agricultural lands and the desire for territorial expansion; their and (our) ancestors battled the Fula forces of the Kingdom of Fouta Djallon.

On arrival, the tribe, more than half of them converted to Islam. But they did not show much resistance while having to give up their indigenous beliefs and accepting the Islamic belief structure. And during the 16th, 17th and 18th century as many as a third of the West African Mandinka population were shipped to the Americas as slaves. As I said before, the Mandinka live primarily in West Africa, particularly in Gambia, Guinea-Bissau, Mali, Sierra Leone, Cote d'Ivoire, Senegal, Burkina Faso, Benin, Liberia, Nigeria, Mauritania and even small communities in the central African nation of Chad. And the Bantu people, of South Africa are also said to be descendents of the Mandinka people. The Mandinka set up home in West Africa and lived harmoniously until the onslaught of slavery. The need for additional farm hands and the initiation of the Industrial Revolution brought many westerners to West Africa. The hunt was for people who submitted easily under pressure and thus, from the 16th century, right through to the 18th century, with the help of Arabian and African tribes which had converted to Islam, more than a third of the Mandinka population was shipped out of West Africa, and this is the reason why almost all African-Americans, West Indians and South American Blacks living in the western hemisphere today are descendents of the Mandinka people.

So I'm going to try and run this down as good as possible and start with the Mandingo psyche... Mandingos I have known and loved but, don't forget that when Jews and Whites considered trading slaves from Africa they looked for tribes that could be easily subdued, and captured. Of course when the slave merchants came looking for slaves, the Arabians and Islamic Mandinka already knew that their brothers would be suitable for this purpose because they had already forced many of them to accept their belief system which many Mandingos in Africa and America still have today which is "Islam". Mind you, there were captives from Nigeria, Ghana, Senegal, Gambia etc. and at least one third of the Mandinka population were brutally captured and forced into slavery by the hands of Jewish, African and Arabian slave traders. The Portuguese, Dutch, Brazilian and American Jews are the perpetrators of the North Atlantic Slave Trade, and they are responsible for the forced capture of many Mandinka tribes living close to Islamic countries near the Sahara, and were shipped out to the Americas, all West Africans. They could not speak each others language, but they were all Mandinka people, hence the same basic mentality...

Now you're probably wondering, what does all this have to do with the relationship and compatibility between Black men and Black women in America, and the answer is everything...

Because it has much to do with the psyche of the Mandinka people in general, and even though Jewish merchants had a hand in shaping our destiny, fact still remains that we as a people are basically intolerant of each other. But Black people, it's not the White mans fault anymore, we have been given enough opportunities to make something out of ourselves and totally get rid of this stigma. Now, if any of you guys and gals out there get a little perturbed about what I'm saying; I really don't give a hoot. I myself am just sick and tired of the BS, especially Black people trying to put the problems and blame where they think they should be rather than where they are, and we have to understand and confront the problems in order to do something about them.

So I would like to reveal to each and every one of us a part of this whole scenario that to my knowledge has not as of yet been touched upon about the "True" nature of the so called Negro (Mandinka) race, who we are, where we comes from, what we do and why we are the way we are. But in order to understand our future we will have to know and understand our past (which most of us don't know) in order to move on. I know, I know, that was then and this is now... I'm only trying to get you to see the reason. But to get a better understanding we are going to look a one hell of an African man who basically brought mass murder to the African continent.

One of the most famous, renowned and feared African worriers and kings in African history was none other than Shaka Zulu. Shaka Zulu brought "Real" warfare to the African nations, but the bottom line is that Shaka Zulu was a vengeful and blood thirsty killer. He also allied himself with many Bantu/Mandinka tribesmen and chieftains. It is generally accepted that the Bantu speaking peoples originated from West Africa around 5,000 years ago in several major waves of migration. And the final southwards migration that took place into the southern regions of Africa, was around 2,000 years ago. And since Shakas reign as king of the Zulu/Bantu almost every country in Africa has been and are still faced with some type or rebellious gangster ready to kill anything that doesn't belong to their tribe or people and take over.

Sierra Leone is a perfect example of Mandingo hatred. Hutu against the Tutsi; the brutality in which innocent people were dismembered and slaughtered like cattle was Mandingo at his best. This is pure Mandingo against Mandingo and has little to do with white folks. But this type of behaviour is present in all Mandinka people living in Africa, North, South, Middle America and the West Indies. North, south, east or west, no matter where you look there is always conflict in Africa but 85% of the time it's in West Africa.

Shaka Zulu introduced mass killing of other tribes during tribal warfare through his campaigns to control all of South Africa. In the old days, it was more or less simulated warfare; when a person from one tribe was killed by someone from another tribe, they fought until they avenged that one death and it was over. But when Shaka Zulu came on the scene that's when all that changed because he didn't stop at only one or two deaths, Shaka Zulu-commander of *"ibutholempi"*(fighting unit) and his men killed tens of thousands. But Shaka Zulu also unwillingly betrayed his people by permitting European settlers to enter and operate in the Zulu kingdom to show his gratitude after Henry Francis Fynn provided medical treatment to the king after an assassination attempt from a rival tribesman hidden in a crowd. This would of course open the door for future British incursions into the Zulu kingdom that were not so peaceful, and you know the rest of the story. Shaka gave new meaning to the word "WAR" and is only one example, but he basically set the tone and many African dictators who have since risen to power has done it through some type of violent takeover and actions against other peoples or each other. But the kicker is-in the end Shaka was assassinated by his own brothers.

I don't know how many of you really know the real Mentality of the African Mandinkan male and female. You know that there is a saying that the apple doesn't fall far from the tree. This is true and I think that we all know what that means. I know and have known many Africans from all parts of Africa, north, south, east and west, and I hope that what I am about to say don't tick anybody off. And if it does, so be it... North, south, east or west, there is too much conflict and animosity among African American males and females. And you can't tell me that this type of behavior has anything to do with the White people; it does NOT! It's in our blood and our genes people, even though most of us do not want to admit it, or actually don't know. So I will try to approach the matter in a more or less sensitive manner and hope that we all can see, understand and connect our behavior to the behavior of the Mandinkan people from whence we come. I need it to be explained to me, I need to know, and the only way for me to understand the present state of mind of Mandinka living in America today is to compare our behavior with that of our ancestors to get the understanding that I seek.

This way I can make a possible connection between Mandingos that live in West Africa and Mandingos that live in America, and show why we as African Americans act the way we do towards each other today. We must try to find some type solution to the problem that most of our people are confronted with all the time but seem to be dormant about it. It doesn't matter if you are a direct descendent, meaning Mandingos that are living in West Africa or indirect meaning Mandingoes living not only in North or South America but the West Indies as well. Africans living in north, south or east Africa could be different, I don't know, but I don't think so. The mentality of killings, rape and violence, is not only in Mandinka people, but in practically all Africans because you still have conflict all over Africa. And of course Coup D'état is very prevalent in almost all West African countries.

Chapter II
Portrait Of The
African Mandinka Male

Sisters, does this sound familiar? Because of his mentality the Mandinka man cats around everywhere having baby after baby with different women, and not taking care of them. I have known and grew to like many African Mandinka men, and there are many inherent traits that they and we (African Americans) all possess. I have known and met many West African men women and children from all types of West African lifestyles from direct descendent of African Kings and Queens to African Juju Priests, this is the truth...

Just to name a few African men that I know well-Kwani *Senegal* Emmu/*Central Africa*, Mweku/*Benin*, George/*Cameroon*, Felix/*Central Africa*, Jacque/*Ivory Coast*, Jojo/*Ghana*, John /*Gambia*, Samuel/*South Africa* and Africans from many different peoples and countries that I can't remember them all-but they all have one trait and that is they all do the same thing. But the Mandinka that I met for the first time in my life that put a sour taste in my mouth from the beginning were Nigerians. This was in 1973 in Frankfurt Germany they were from Hamburg; I had met them earlier that year while performing at a night club called the Fabrik in Hamburg. But anyway a few months later I received a call from them asking me if they could stay at my flat until they could fly out of Frankfurt to Nigeria... Reluctantly I agreed because they said that it would be only for 2 days but wined up staying 4 or 5 days... You know me, always trying to help a brother (that's the way I use to be) today it's a different story-you live and learn... They were truly down and out, with only a flight ticket. So, I had given them money for cigarettes, they ate my food, I gave them a place to sleep and one day they just up and left, poof gone!!! I had been on a gig in Mannheim and when I got back home, them Mandingo niggers were gone, and you know the rest of the story... No thank you, no goodbye, no "kismerass", nada. This of course put a bad taste in my mouth for African men. Never forget; most Africans, male or female will try to use you for their own personal gain, the same as niggers in America, and in case you don't know this, African women do NOT like African American women.

And all you sisters out there, if you are thinking about marrying an African man, you better think twice, because every time you visit his family you have to go bearing gifts for the whole damn clan, usually around 50 Mandingos or so, and make sure that wherever he comes from that they do not practice Polygamy. In many African cultures this practice is normal, and through my many, many years of experience dealing with African men I can tell you this; African men live in many relationships. Even Kweku (Name change) who is a good friend of mine from Benin and works with me sometimes, told me just some time ago that he has brothers and sisters that live in Paris that he don't really know. Even though his father was a diplomat from Benin, he had many children from different women not only in Benin but in at least 4 other African countries as well. Now I'm thinking DAMN... Ironically Kweku is the same as his father;

he has children in Frankfurt, Hanau, and other cities in Germany and Europe, and he actually manifests that which his father did. But Kweku is not the only case. Almost all West African men that I know do this; they cat around and have baby, after baby and are not taking care of them, the same way African American men do. And in many cases these guys are married to at least 2 or 3 different women all at the same time, so you know what that means. This is a tradition that has been going on in Africa for many centuries, the guys lay around the whole day doing nothing and the women have to wait on them. Mandingo is always sitting on his butt, and does not care if his women has to fetch the fire wood, cook the meals, get water, dig for roots, milk the cow, plow the fields, feed the goats and have his babies. In other words she has to carry everything on her back, (girl I know yall know what I'm talking bout) she is the backbone of the family, and the exact same applies to the African American Mandinka women.

The greatest past time of most West African men is to sit around under the old Baobab tree being useless and impregnating their women knowing fully well that they don't have the means to provide for them and their children. You don't have any water because it hasn't rained for 10 years, the livestock is dying, there is no vegetation, you're hungry-under these conditions how can you thing about having sex or babies??? Even wild animals have enough sense to know that if living conditions are not right, not to have offspring. But the most bazaar thing to me is African time; Africans dance to a different drum beat when it comes to time- let's say that you want to meet up with an African man around 12 o'clock noon; you have to tell him to come at 12 o'clock <u>Central European Time,</u> not African time, because if you don't, they will definitely NOT show up before 3 or 4 o'clock in the afternoon-maybe later. Now don't that remind you of niggers at home? Some of my African friends use to say that the sun moves differently in Africa, and that in

Europe they get confused about the real time. But they will come, just not when you want them to; the same way that negroes do in America. You know, the White man has always said that Blacks people are lazy; with that he meant Mandingos and Mandingorettes. He was right then and still is, but he himself is also lazy, he could have picked his own damn cotton. You see that all over Africa and America, or haven't you noticed??? Almost all of the men just lay around all day and let the woman do the work and take care of them; that is the Mandinkan male chauvinistic mentality; oh he'll get up every once in a while and go out to hunt something, but basically he's sitting on his butt expecting his woman to take care of him. And even up until today this type mentality is still that which is keeping many Mandinka men and women down, because not too much has changed since we were abducted.

This type of mentality and behaviour has been handed down to Mandingos in America by our West African ancestors for generations, and here we are in the "New World", we can't speak the language or communicate with each other, but our mentality, psychological makeup, distrust and hatred for each other that we inherited form our forefathers has manifest itself into what it is today and is becoming a key factor in the destruction of the Mandingo slave.

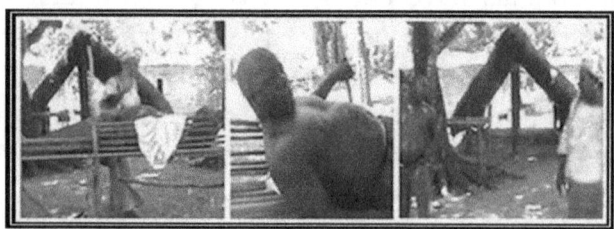

Note:
This is typical Mandingo mentality-sleeping under the Baobab tree all day long and when his wife wakes his lazy AZ up he wants to fight her. Blacks in America are exactly the same, it's just that we don't have a Baobab tree.

Another trait is that the African man allows the White man to come into his country and exploit all of their natural resources for only a few pennies, and because of Mandingo's tenacious nature he naturally wants everything for himself, taking hundreds of millions, knowing all the time that his people are starving and dying, or they sell millions of diamonds to support their wars and aggressions against themselves and other West African nations.

Chapter III

Portrait Of The
African Mandinka Female

Mandinkan women

Many Blacks in America have absolutely no idea as to what is happening in the rest of the world. The African woman is the salt of the earth, this is where it all began-a slave to her man, she has to go out in the wilderness and gather food, which includes searching for roots, gathering berries, or anything edible. She has to take care of the cows, sheep, goats, fetch water and have his babies. She has practically no voice, and depending on the tribe in most cases does not own anything. But on the other hand has to try and make sure that her family is cared for and basically by and means necessary because her lazy AZ good for nothing Mandingo man is sitting on his butt under the Baobab tree talking crap and signifying or sleeping.

Often her man is not at home, but out somewhere in another town, village, country or neighbourhood living with or even married to other women that has his children which she is aware of. Usually there is practically no social systems set up in her country to help them in any way at all, so they are forced to live the lives that they live and there is practically nothing that they can do about it.

But as we all know, many West African women are starving and having many complications with giving birth because they have nothing to eat and life is hell. In America that is not the case. Even though many Black women live below or at the poverty line in America, they still have much, much more than the average African woman. And with all of this, they also have to cope with their men running around impregnating as many women as they can to prove their manhood. She has to sit and wait for month at a time before she hears anything from him at all, or he finally decides to come home from his escapades. African women are very much aware of what their men are doing, they know that he has many women in different cities in Africa and any place that he can. And she continues to put up wit his BS even though she knows that there is little hope that he will ever change. On the other hand they are not all like this, I do know West African men who are dedicated to their wives and families. Even in her own country the African woman has to endure rape, murder, and many forms of Black-on-Black violence and crime that is so prevalent in most of West Africa- being brutally assaulted and demeanoured, they have to live through all the Bokassas, the Idi Amins, the General Buck Naked's, the children soldier's and still try to retain some type of dignity in their God forsaken country.

But I must also say that many African men leave their country of course in search of a better life someplace else, especially in Europe, and when they go back home they are expected to bring gifts and money back with them for all members of the family. They are expected to and most do send money back to their families; this is the main reason I think many African women tolerate this type behaviour. This is also part of the reason why Mandingos in America always have their hands out, gimme, gimme, gimme, especially the chicken eating preachers, and they never think that they are responsible for their own lives. Many African women that you find in Europe are illiterate and have no aspects of finding a job, so they are forced to rely on the man to support them, whether husband or son. Even if they do make it to Europe, they usually go into prostitution because by not being able to read or write it's almost impossible to find a job.

Chapter IV
Portrait Of The
African American Mandinka Male

Hardly any White person anyplace knows how is it to be discriminated against, and this includes the entire world. In the old days, Black men in the south had to act like White women didn't exist, they would never look them straight in the eye, because if he acted differently he ran the risk of being lynched or put in jail. The Black mans world was and is flooded with White women, the media, news papers, magazines, radio, television, and now the internet all bring these "Lilies" to bloom, and the Black man found and still find it difficult to separate his idea of an "Ideal" woman from that of the White woman. That is one of the main reasons why many Black men seek light colored (high yellow) or Mulatto Black women. Because of the taboos of desiring a White woman, she (the Black woman) is still Black and thus not as good as a "REAL" White woman. And these "High Yellow" half white Mandingos are preferred by many Black men, even though she is not white but high yellow she incites and strikes awe in them, which brings them closer to white. The White man has always said and still say that Black men have always had that savage urge to sleep with a White woman. And in many cases this is true, but it is also a by product of what Jim Crow and other racist American bigots were about, and anything white south of the Mason Dixon Line you better leave alone. But the truth of the matter is, that it's not only the Mandingos that want to be with Becky, Becky also wants to be with Mandingo as well.

During slavery times Jews and White men treated Black men like the animals they themselves were, and they have always tried to justify their brutality against the Black man in whatever way was convenient for them. And there were basically two types of slaves, the house slave and the filed slave, and being a field slave was not at all easy. A field slave worked from sunrise to sunset, but during harvest time, they worked an eighteen our day, and women worked the same hours as the men; and if they were pregnant they worked up until the baby was born. After the child was born the mother worked with the baby on her back. The field workers lived in small huts with a dirt floor which was absolutely no protection against the cold weather; and using the scarce rough blankets and straw that they had to sleep on they endured the long cold winter months.

The field slaves basically worked the tobacco fields and cotton fields, planting, harvesting, binding and stacking from sunup to sundown, but they also had to do all the chores which went with owning a plantation. Slaves had to pick a minimum of 200 lbs of cotton a day in order to receive their daily food rationing; even though slaves were driven the whole day by the overseers with whips, during their free time the slaves would supplement their food by fishing and hunting. Usually at the age of twelve a child's work became almost the same as an adult's. Even though the house slaves were living under somewhat better conditions they were not much. They had to clean, cook, serve meals, and take care of the masters children. Some house slaves lived in attics, closets, or corners in the big house even if their families lived in the slave quarters. Anyway, when the Jewish merchants took us out of Africa (and believe me, I ain't mad with you), we brought with us all of the traits and attitudes that the Mandinka people possessed and had inherited from their ancestors. This mentality and the techniques the White slave masters used helps me explain why many, way too many Black males in America are the way they are, mindless decedent degenerates of society. Mind you I am not trying to make excuses for their (our) behaviour, but it will explain some things to you.

The average Black American Mandingo male, what does he do? He follows the footsteps of his ancestral fathers and sit around all day doing nothing, he learns at a very early age how to do nothing, because he has hardly any Black male roll models to keep him focused and keep him going in the right direction. He lets his woman, or his mother take care of him. His mother is a single parent and has little control over him and he causes her nothing but heartaches and pain. She still has that natural fear for his life because the slave masters have driven this into her for so many years. Many of these little nappy headed Mandingos become fathers at very early ages. They cat around in the hood having sex with as many girls and women as they can, and when the girls get pregnant they make themselves scarce. He will not try to make an honest living by working because he thinks that selling dope on the street is more profitable and the hip thing to do. Usually he drops out school at an early age and by doing this he adds to the problems which he is unaware of that he faces. He tries to blame the White man for his dilemma, but don't realize that he himself is responsible for his destination and or future. It has gotten to the point where young Black males in many cities throughout the United States of America don't expect to live past their 18th birthday. Why? Because of the Black-on-Black crime that has swept the nation. Black men are the #1 killers of Black men, and of course by them doing this, it pleases the White man because he don't have to do it anymore.

During slavery, Jews and White people tried to and took our pride; pride as humans and as people and cross bread us like mules. The so called African Negro slave was kept in bondage until the emancipation of the Mandinka people on January 1, 1863. Even then of course the harassment, scare tactic and the killings continued up until today! The Negro male had no choice but to conform to their demands, they had all the whips, all the guns, the law and all the other white decadents that helped them keep their niggers in line. It's truly a sad chapter in Black-Jewish-White relations, because it shows what decadent b......s they really are, and every time I think about it I want to f..k somebody up. But when the Black man got weapons that's when things started to change.

Black males started to fight back using their (the White man) own weapons against them; before that time Negroes could only retaliate by running away, so that's what they did. To show how scared they were, Black men had to endure the rape and torture of his woman through the hands of Jewish and White men and couldn't do anything about it. Whites were beating Blacks barbarically. They seldom killed them, but on occasions they would take the biggest and most unruly buck whip, and tar and feather him. And anybody that can come up with something like this is a diabolical, devious, murderous scum invertebrate excuse for a human being. This is truly unbelievable and they try to say that Blacks are savages, that might be true but Whites are Barbaric and demonic murderers.

They beat the men women and children, morning noon and night, and of course this had a tremendous effect on the psyche of the Mandingo people, males and females, especially the males.

This is partly the reason why Blacks use to and still whip their children, because they had been whipped themselves as children and their parents and grand parents were whipped and beaten by the White degenerate pigs. But believe it or not, Africans do NOT whip their children, you will hardly ever see this. But the turn of the century didn't help the Black males one bit, by then the Industrial Revolution was taking a turn, and it would still be very difficult for Black males; and to find a job was almost impossible because the oppression and scare tactics that the White man used continued on especially in the south.

Proud Black Men

One method that the white supremacist pigs used to control Black males was lynching, they also tarred and feathered them and ripped them apart with horses, just to name a few things. And violence in the United States of America against African Americans, especially in the south, rose during the aftermath of the civil war after slavery had been abolished and recently freed Black men and women were given the right to vote. Violence rose even more at the end of the century, after southern white Democrats regained Political power in the South in the 1870s. And most Southern States passed new constitutions or legislation which effectively disenfranchised most Blacks and many poor Whites, established segregation of public facilities by race, and separated Blacks from the most common public facilities. Nearly 5,000 African Americans men were lynched and slaughtered in the United States between 1860 and1890. The 1900s gave rise to Blacks in sports, and this boosted the Black mans confidence a little by the admission of Blacks in sports-great boxers such as **Joe** (The Brown Bomber) **Louis**, who knocked out all the great white hopes world champions in this order-*Primo Carnera*, the great German heavyweight *Max Baer, Jack Sharkey James J. Braddock,* and of course the great German "white hope" and world champion, *Max Schmeling* whom Joe Louis knocked completely out in the first round. Joseph Louis Barrow better known as *Joe Louis*, was the world heavyweight boxing champion from 1937 to 1949. He is considered to be one of the greatest heavyweights of all time.

Nicknamed the ***Brown Bomber***, Louis helped elevate boxing from the lowest point of it's popularity in the post-Jack Dempsey era by establishing a reputation as an honest, hardworking fighter at a time when the sport was dominated by gambling interests. All in all, Joe successfully defended his title victoriously in 25 bouts, which was a record for the heavyweight division. In 2005, Joe Louis was named the greatest heavyweight of all time by the International Boxing Research Organization, and was ranked number one on *The Ring*'s list of the 100 Greatest Punchers of All Time. Joe Louis is widely regarded as the first African American to achieve the status of a nationwide hero within the United States of America, and was also a focal point of anti-Nazi sentiment leading up to and during World War II. He also was instrumental in breaking the color barrier in Golf by appearing under a sponsor's exemption in a PGA event in 1952.

Or ***Sugar Ray Robinson*** the greatest middle weight champion to enter a boxing ring knock out more men than any other boxer. Some of his victims were *Jake LaMotta, Randy Turnipt, Joey Maxim, Gene Fullmer, Carmen Basilio, Jean Stock,* just to name a few. Born in 1920 in Detroit Michigan as Walker Smith Jr. (sugar Ray) borrowed his name, and as a boy he would watch Joe Louis work out; the two actually liked each other and Louis would let Ray carry his gloves into the gym, where Ray learned and watched the champ go through his motions. By borrowing the name Ray Robinson from a friend boxer that he knew that was 16 years old, he was able get past the checkers because the minimum age for fighters was 16 years. Sugar Ray won his first match at the tender young age of 14 for a $17 watch, and he knocked his opponent out cold. Sugar Ray was not only king of the middle weight he was also king of the welterweight boxers. Henry Armstrong and Fritzie Zivic are two great welterweights and Sugar Ray beat them both. Walker Smith Jr. (sugar Ray Robinson) is the greatest boxer that ever put on a pair of gloves-he has a long list of bouts starting with Jack LaMotta who he fought 6 times, Randy Turnip, Gene Fuller, and Carmen Basilio. Even though he failed in his bid to get the Light Heavyweight title because of heat exhaustion, he was forced to forfeit the title to Joey Maxim as a KO. He knocked out Bobo Olsen, and Jean Stock in Paris just to name a few. Now these are all White boys you know... And the brothers were kicking those White carcasses getting back for some of some of the crap the White man did to our ancestors and are still doing to us today. Now you know when they did that, Mandingos all over America were going crazy.

Jack Johnson (master technician) was certainly one of the most celebrated heavy weight boxers to enter a ring was an all-around star fighter. He not only had the best uppercut, he was the best defensive fighter, the best counter puncher, and the master of feinting. Many boxing experts picked Jack Johnson as the greatest heavy weight of all times, he was not only the greatest defensive fighter but equally good on offense. *John Arthur Johnson,* born 1894 in Galveston, Texas was given the nickname "Lil Arthur" as a boy because he was small and frail. But after a spurt of growth in his teens which transformed him form a frail boy to a giant of a young man when he was around

16 years old. He enjoyed sports and his favourite was of course boxing, his daily routine included shadow boxing, feinting, weaving and throwing punches which he became a master at. He learned early in life that competing in sports with whites was virtually impossible for a Black man because of the generally accepted racial beliefs of both blacks and whites. After much time and patience he had polished his style to perfection; he finally got the chance at the title after he had been fighting in the Negro league for over nine years. Johnson was convinced that the "big black bucks" should have been fighting Whites and not Blacks. Jack Johnson was a flamboyant Black man that loved White women and had many of them which of course angered all of the white supremacist.

The Australian government believed that prize fighting had no color barriers, and any champion that refused to challenge a worthy opponent was a coward and should not be a champion. He finally became world champion after humiliating the racist heavyweight champion of the white boxing world Tommy Burns who had called Johnson "yellow" and many other racial slurs. Johnson purposely kept the bout going to give racist Burns the AZ whipping of his life, and to prove to white folks, that you are not all that. The only thing that saved Burns was the fact that the Australian police intervened and stopped the bout.

Wilma Rudolf - *The First Woman Ever To Run And Win 3 Olympics Gold Medals.* From Polio to Gold Medalist - Wilma Rudolph made Olympic history by becoming the first woman, not to mention the first African American woman, to win three gold medals. Wilma Rudolph was born in 1940, in Saint Bethlehem Tennessee. Wilma struggled most of her childhood trying to beat the devastations of Polio. Wilma Rudolph was born into a very large, poor, African-American family; she was the twentieth of twenty two children.

Europe Rome, Italy: September 7, 1960, Olympic track and field winter games. Wilma Rudolph's accomplishments in track and field-taking first place in both the 100-meter and 200-meter dash and in the 4x100 relay-opened the door for women and girls in a previously all-male track and field events. Graceful, elegant fast and slender, the Italian press called her (LaGazelle) the Gazelle.

James Cleveland Owens defied racial bias and humiliation with his running and jumping skills to gain a college education at Ohio State University. "Jesse" Owens was an African American track and field athlete who specialized in the sprints and the long jump. He participated in the 1936 Summer Olympics in Berlin Germany, where he achieved international fame by winning four gold medals; one each in the 100 meters, 200 meters, long jump and as part of the 4x100 meter relay team. He was the most successful athlete at the 1936 Summer Olympics. *Jesse Owens* is remembered as one of the most outstand sport figures of his time, left his impact on Black athletes and non athletes for 3 generations. At the Olympic games in 1936 he surpassed himself not only achieving victory but also winning 4 gold medals, and in many parts of the south he was hailed as a great hero, he shattered Adolf Hitler's boasting of White Arian supremacy, and became one of Americas greatest ambassador for sports.

Black Music

And on the music scene during the 40s and 50s of course Black musicians had and still have the lead in producing different music styles-greats such as Fats Waller, Scott Joplin king of Ragtime, Louis Armstrong king of Dixie, Count Basie big band, Duke Ellington A Train. Not only did you have great composers you also had great soloist such as Lester Young, Charlie (yard bird) Parker, Dizzy Gillespie and Miles Davis, Herschel Evans, Harry (Sweets Edison) Eddy (Lock jaw) Davis, Sonny Rollins, and many more all leading the way and making Black music what it is today.

This also gave Black males a small boost in confidence, but they still had to be careful with their actions because the White man still had all the guns, and the law on his side. This went on all way up to the 1960s and at this time Mandingos were really up in a frenzy... Martin Luther King was on the non-violent trip while Malcolm X and the Black Panthers were saying "by any means necessary".

Blackman in the 60s

But in the 60s there was also a big split in the community, some Blacks were taking the non-violent approach and were following Dr. Martin Luther kings lead, by marching in the streets in the southern hemisphere of the continental United States of America. As we all know Dr. King advocated a non-violent approach to social equality in America, which caused his death and the death of many Blacks living in this part of America. During this time you actually saw the true raw hatred and anger that Whites, especially White males had and still have for Black people, especially Black males. But the killing part is, Black people living in any part of the world have never done anything to or against White people. So how do you explain all this hatred that you have? No one has done anything to you, but being White, no one has to; do they?

The 60s also ushered in a new renaissance in African American music, with New Wave Jazz and a new HOT FUNKY beat hit us with James Brown, the Supremes, the Temptations, Chuck Berry, Isley Brothers and many great Black artist and musicians. Even on up to the modern day Hip Hop, Mandingos have always been the leaders in modern pop music, and always will be. And by the time the 80s rolled around, Blacks and Whites had at least started to respect each other a little more even though White men were still harassing and killing niggers.

I don't know if you noticed it or not but, the White man always try to blame and hang everything on Mandingo; if anything went wrong the nigger did it, and they try to say that we are angry, well, hell yeah we are angry, wouldn't you be? After all it was YOUR idea to start the slavery system in America in the first place. We have a right to be angry because first of all you steal many of our ideas, music, dance, life style, and say that they are your own. Sure Blacks are angry, we are angry because America was NOT build on your backs alone; many Black men and women have sacrificed their lives for the American dream in times of peace and war. On the other hand the Black Panther Party said that you have to fight fire with fire, and as we all know by this time Blacks had armed themselves. The Revolution will not be televised it will be *LIVE!* was the Slogan.

The Angry Black Man

And since I can't figure out what makes White people so racist, I can only assume that it is jealously. Maybe this is the reason why many Whites are afraid of or sometimes act as though they are afraid of Blacks, men and women. But it's something and it's not because of the way we look, because if that was the case then why do they try to get as black as they can by lying in the sun all day because you can't stand your white skin? And many White men are jealous and afraid of the Black mans strong personality, why? Hell I don't know, but it's unfounded that's for sure.

Because a White man will kill you just as quick as a Black man will, maybe even quicker. Black men have reason and the right to be angry because first of all, you prevent us from participating in the community as full human beans and because of all of the BS that you have been saying about us, the way you have purposely killed and injured many of our people, the way you lie to get what you want, the raping of our women and daughters, the oppression, the hatred; take it all and put it all together and you can call that anger- yes we have a right to be angry. After all it is the 21st century and you still can't give any real reason why you act as YOU do. We have a right to be angry for all the beatings, and the Kinta Kuntas, the tar and featherings, the hangings; yes we are angry-at least I am... We are angry because you bring tons of narcotics into our community and neighborhoods which automatically causes crime and with the help of other Mandingos influence our young people to start using drugs and narcotics. And this also contributes to the constant problem of Black on Black crime. We are ticked off about housing, jobs and social welfare; and you know if you take social welfare from niggers that there would definitely be an uprising, and Black women would be on the front line. Contrary to popular belief, we, American Mandingo males, are just like almost all West African Mandinka men. We lay around all day blaming the White man for being brought to the land of plenty. We are lazy and make excuses while our women take care of us, the baby, earn the money, buy the food, cook the food, get the kids ready for school, (in most cases) feed the dog and the chickens, and have our babies. The African American male does exactly the same thing as his African counterpart. They cat around and have baby, after baby, after baby, not taking care of them and leading double lives with many women and children. This has been going on in America for years now, just as in Africa, and all of the gang warfare, killings and all that BS, we inherited form our African ancestors. It's a case of slavery in freedom.

This is something that is totally unprecedented in many other races. And the White man knew and took advantage of the inherent quality that we have to brutalize each other. Mandingos seem to forget one thing, and that is that you are Black and the average White man does not want to have anything to do with you. This type behaviour is in almost all races, even those poor bastards in India or South America think that they are better than Blacks-especially Black men, and as far as most of them are concerned Black people are dwelling at the bottom of the Totem Pole... But not everybody hate Blacks, Greeks, Turks, Italians, Vietnamese, Thai-I know for sure that in general these people truly have absolutely no problems with Blacks, and I know for sure that Turkish and Greek men have high respect and esteem for Afro American men. Now I'm talking about European Greeks and Turks and Italians, because they have not been swayed by the ways of the American colonist pig. I can only say that since I have been on my world tour, I am able to see the situation through different eyes. And when you are directly involved with something, sometimes you can't see the forest for the trees.

Many prominent Black actors and entertainers are following the foot steps of many before them such as Sydney Poitier who incidentally was the first Black man to win an Academy award, or Sammy Davis Jr. for instance have almost always gone to the other side of the fence. Even as far back as Friedrich Douglas-and we all know that Jack Johnson was one of the most famous boxers to hit the ring had 3 white wives. There are only a few Black actors like Denzel Washington or Samuel L. Jackson or directors like Spike Lee that have Black women. Even many of our NFL Big Black Bucks that were being pitted against each other during slavery are getting on the band wagon. I think that it's BS to want to be like the man that is keeping many Black men down. And Black people men and women throughout the world don't know their worth, why? Because we have lost our identity, and it has been taken away from us by the Jew, White man, West African Mandinka and Arabian people. You know there is a lot of information out there and I could write a book on this subject alone, but it's not about writing a lot of words, it's about telling our people what problems we are facing and seeking workable solutions to solve them. The American dream-that's what it's all about, and anybody can achieve their dreams despite their background. Right? Wrong...Because even though the White man has given us many privileges and granted us more or less access to the community, the government and the police are still contributing to our dilemma. Even though I say that the problem is not totally the White mans fault anymore, he still discriminates against us, especially through the justice and penal system which still put us at a disadvantage, because it is much more difficult if you are a young Black man living in America today. And if you are, you are more than likely to be killed by Black-on-Black violence than anything else. If you survive your teens, you're more than likely to be arrested than a young White person, you are more likely to have a harsher sentence passed against you than a White offender, you are more likely to be incarcerated, and far less likely to find a job than a White person whether you have a prison record or not.

Black Crime

The racial composition of the US population as of 2008 was 79.79% White American 14.19% Hispanic, 12.84% African American 4.45% Asian American. The relationship between race and crime in the United States has been a topic of public controversy and scholarly debate for many decades now. Since the 1980s, the debate has been centered around the causes of and contributing factors but not the origin. The Census Bureau breaks it down into Blacks and Hispanic Blacks, but we are all descendents of Mandinkan people, and according to the US Bureau of Justice Statistics, non-Hispanic Blacks accounted for 30.4% of the prison and jail population in 2009. Also according to the Bureau of Justice Statistics from 2000 to 2008 there was a decline in the rate of incarceration for Blacks to 3,161 per 100,000 and the White rate slightly increased to 487 per 100,000.

Despite the decrease we are according to reports still 6 times more likely to be incarcerated for the same crime that Whites commit, and our Black leaders don't give a hoot, from the president on down to the most minor senator. For men in their early thirties, African Americans are about 7 times more likely to have a prison record and conviction than Whites. 22% are more likely to have been in prison, in comparison to 17% enlisting in the military.

According to stats, there are close to 800,000 Black men in jail as compared to a little more than 600,000 Black men in college. At 4.8% Blacks have a higher incarceration rate than the 1.9% that Hispanic have and the 0.7% Whites have. Black-on-Black crime is the biggest threat to the stability that we as African Mandinka face today. The stats are through the roof, and there seems to be no relief in sight. But I'm sorry to have to always say this, but I can only attribute it to 2 things, Black man Black woman, and of course that all too familiar Mandingo self hatred that continuously cause us to disrespect and kill each other.

Black On Black Crime

While African Americans comprise only 13% of the total U.S. Population, 43% of all murder victims in 2007 were African American and 93.1% of those killed, were killed by other African Americans. Victimizations of African Americans from violent crime include the following: homicide, rape, sexual assault, robbery, theft, aggravated and simple assault which was 24% in 2007 and the highest percentage rate in America. But the impact affects us all. It is social, political, psychological and economic. Each year, nearly 4.5 billion dollars are spent on healthcare related to violence. It affects all of our communities, regardless of racial composition. The people affected by Black-on-Black crime are not just statistics that you read about everyday in your newspaper. They are fathers, mothers, brothers, sisters, cousins sons and daughters, neighbours, co-workers, church goers and everyone in the community. No matter how safe you think your own neighbourhood is, no part of our community is completely safe, and the effects are grim, long-lasting and undeniable because Black-on-Black crime is real and it hits us all right in the heart.

Bloods gang member   Robbery   Crips gang member

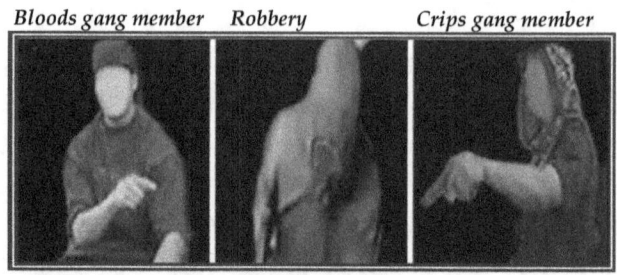

Gang related crime should definitely be the one #1 priority, and according to the "National Youth Gang Survey Analysis" (2009) which states that gangs in America are comprised of 49% are Hispanic, 35% are African-American, 9% Caucasian, and 7% are other race or ethnicity. Shockingly, though Black people make up only 13 percent of the American population, a third of all Black men aged 20-29 are in prison, on probation, or on parole right now. And it's a terrible thing when a child thinks that the gang is more important than their own families; of course they feel safe and secure in the gang, but this is definitely the wrong type of security for a 15 year old. Bloods, Cripps, it's a most terrible thing when your life is dependent on the colors that you wear. What we need to do in America first of all is to get rid of these Black gangs and gangsters, and do it by any means necessary; but the only way that this can happen is to be a hands on parent, and prevent your child from participating in these gangs and gang activities.

Gangs are one of the biggest threats to our young people even more than drugs because, less gangs equate to less drugs which means less killings and murders, because we all know that many of these killings are gang and drug related; but unfortunately our youth are lazy just as we are and they think that by robbing and killing and taking what others have is normal. And these video cops and robbers games that they play today, are especially geared towards Black-on-Black crime, because the images are many times of Blacks and Black kids are playing these killer take all games causing the child to become more violent. They teach Black kids to wage war on each other, not knowing that these games are created by the White man to help destroy the Black man. So all you punk "negras" out there, pull up your pants because the only thing that you are doing is showing your AZ nothing more... Even though we have gained some type of respect from the White man, he still basically has control over us because he controls everything and has used every conceivable method to control Blacks that he could think of. And one way to do this is through the courts and the police. The police are the force that will help control the niggers, and as we all know the American police force leaves a lot to be desired.

Police Brutality

But you have to realize now that even in our court system the jurors were always White, if a Black person was being tried for a crime just as in many cases today, the Black man would always be found guilty; so you had not only the police brutality against you, but the courts and the White jurors that convicted Blacks as well.

What the cops didn't do, the penal system did the rest to finish us off. Giving Whites lesser sentences than Blacks for the same crime-we all know this. Today White cops kill many Blacks and taser Whites to death and get away with it; even if the killing was video taped by five different people they will still be set free. The police are being trained more and more that the general public is their enemy, and Afro-Americans are to receive "special treatment"...

The enemy (us citizens) can now be engage with outright brutality without recourse or any action taken against them. An epidemic of police violence and brutality has swept America, and the president and all the American politicians are going along with it.

The order to use "pain compliance", which is just another name for police torture and brutality, was given the police to subdue and suppress American citizens. America has become a tyrannical police state where the cops don't even have respect for an 80 year old woman, and spray maze in the face of a 5 year old Black girl and the government is on their side. But I must say that in many cases the Black police officer is more brutal to Blacks than White officers are. This is really screwed up... And if you watch footage where cops are beating a Black person, most of the time there are Black officers involved. Many people are saying that the president should get more involved, and try and do something about the situation, well I say the same thing, but on the other hand, why should the president be the only one to have to speak up for the Black mans plight in America, especially as far as police brutality is concerned? We have hundreds of Black politicians and officials, many in high positions such as the honourable Judge Alan Page for instance, why are they not speaking up? Sure they're in a different category but after all they are still Black Mandinka men. If you as a Black man are interested in White women, that's ok, but don't forget who you are, where you came from and where you're going. I'm not advocating separation of the races, but in my opinion many Black men are afraid to face the truth about themselves, and that is why the White man has made a mule out of you and the only way that you can retaliate is to try and become like him by seeking that White flesh instead of trying to get a decent education. Incidentally this is one big reasons why Black women are dating White men, because the educational standard and level of the Black man in most cases does not compare up to hers.

These types of Black men in my opinion are only degenerates who are playing out their desires to help his White slave master control others, especially members of his own race.

Mandinka men have been betraying their race as far back as the 13th century when West Africans aided the Arabians in capturing and converting many Mandinka people to Islam. This is in our blood. That is why the White man had it so easy when taming the beast. This of course helps me explains why all these Mandingo punks are uploading on the internet all this BS about sisters. The African Mandinka male at that time had already started the ball rolling by deceiving his people to get an advantage over them. Mankind has always had some form of communication; back then "Mandingo" used none other that the "Drum" to communicate with each other to let the captors know where their brothers were and what they were doing, and today it's the media and the internet.

But when Black people simulate Black-on-Black crime and violence on the internet, this is not helping our cause in any way what so ever, and are adding to the problem of how others see us; even though many of the videos that I have viewed are not real and the participants are only acting out this type violence for others to see on the internet are just shining a bad light on Black people.

These Mandingos are only opportunist, disgusting in their manner and only trying to advance their own cause at the expense of others by acting out these scenes of Black-on-Black crime and violence. And I've even seen Asians and Europeans calling each other "Nigger", and that's only because Blacks use this word to refer to each other; but because the influence and impact of Black men, especially Black musicians and athletics is so big on other cultures, many young people want to do that what Blacks do and be like them, the way we dress, act and the whole nine yards.

Chapter V
Portrait Of The African American Mandinka Woman

Blacks, Indians, Jews, Poles, Mexicans, Asian, you name it, minorities in America have always been brutalized and victimized by the White man, his evil mind and deeds such as, discrimination, prejudices, injustices, persecution, murder and down right blood thirsty ways and hatred. But the one who has suffered the most under the hands of the Godless and diabolical sub-human White men has been none other than the Black woman. The sexual atrocities that Black women had to endure in the United States of America north and south, have done more to damage her personality than one can imagine. "HE" mated with the beast which he dehumanized and fathered the children that according to their philosophy were "without souls", and took them and made slaves out of them to be sold on slave auctions and taken away from their mothers. That literally shows you that they had no morals, not even when it came to his own blood. Why? Because they considers the Black woman a slut and whore, and everything that she bore was less than human, but he mated with her just the same. Out of the darkened canals of White and Jewish inhumanity to Black women in America their epitaph has yet to be written. And after tens of decades of being raped, murdered, beaten, spat upon, denied human respect, treated like sluts and mammies only fit to suckle and nurture White babies, to wash, to scrub, clean, sweat, sexually demoralized, and taken for the having; Black women have finally come to realize that they are women with their own sexual desires, and American citizens with rights and longings just like any other citizens in the republic for which it stands. That only shows you that the White man puts himself above God. How can he think that a woman that is so close to God, that he in his superiority can treat the mother of Jesus in this manner? Because I personality have never read anything in the Bible that makes reference to White women, or man during biblical times.

In 2011 the African American woman, finds herself in the exact same dilemma as she did 300 years ago, and 300 years later she is still mirroring that what the West African Mandinka woman have been doing for centuries. And the African American Mandinka woman has basically the same mentality as that of the African Mandinka woman. Difference being basically geographically. From Africa into slavery, throughout bondage and up to the so called emancipation of the Negro slave the Black woman in America has always had to keep things together in order to save and provide for her family. The roll of the Black woman in America has almost always been one of the bread winner in the family simply because during slavery the Black man was stripped of his natural instinct to protect his woman. And after the emancipation proclamation, Whites refused to give Black men jobs. Simple as that... At that time, as far as Whites were concerned Black males were only good for picking cotton, lynching and getting whipped. And every time I think about that it makes my hair rise. The Black woman has always had to stand up for the Black man, she was less oppressed than he was, but still oppressed. When the slave masters beat us into a pulp, she tended our wounds and she had to endure rape, demeaning and immoral treatment under the White and Jewish male supremacist, and couldn't do anything about it.

African American women are not much different from their counterparts living in West Africa. Many of them are not educated, they have baby after baby and can't afford to care of them, and way too many of them are too busy trying to get money from the social welfare system to take care of themselves and their children instead of trying to get an education or find a decent job to provide for their families, especially if they are single mothers. Or not get pregnant in the first place. The thing would be to have a comprehensive program for young Black women, but by the time many of them reach 20 years of age they already have 3 or 4 kids out of wedlock and by different men.

But that doesn't take away from the fact that the Black woman in America has almost always been the bread winner of the family. And as we all know, often times, that good for nothing Mandingo of hers (her baby daddy) is too busy catting around someplace else. He is out somewhere in his or another neighbourhood selling drugs, or doing some other stupid thing that he should not be doing. African women on the other hand don't have this luxury because most African governments will not help it's citizens. So they are just out there and the man is not helping either. I'm not saying that the system is bad just that many Black women in America are lazy and they are satisfied with the system and the lifestyle they live. Many would rather take their chances on welfare not realizing that when her kids become adults and she is in her 40s with no education, that her life will change for the worse because after the kids are grown, the welfare checks stop. And after that, then what?? They find some way to remain on welfare at least to get their food stamps and anything else that they can get from the system, and by doing it this way they are also teaching their daughter to do the exact same thing as they and become permanently dependent on welfare system.

Black women in America are also victims of the African (Mandinka) Syndrome, they start at an early age having babies, and because they can't find a job and take care of 2 or 3 children at the same time, they go on welfare and usually this is when that Mandingo mentality really set in, meaning simply that they get comfortable with that lifestyle and are on welfare for the rest of their lives. Some of them make it, some don't, plain and simply; and the respect that many young Black women in America have for themselves is dwindling at an accelerated pace. But the question for me is why do Black women always say that they don't want any money from their men to help support their children after the break up? I can understand that you are angry because you have been hurt and I also know that many Black women are too proud, and say "I don't want anything at all from him". Now, this is for me a very stupid mindset and statement, because this type of woman does not realize that she is not hurting the man but her children.

So sisters wake up! You are making your child suffer because of your stupid behaviour, make that Mandingo step up to the plate and take care of his "churen", you as a mother owe it to your child. But sisters you are not 100% free of guilt in this situation… But this is minor in comparison to what Black men are about and becoming more of. First of all we as Black men need to recognize the fact that Black women are the most beautiful woman in the world. All the colours and shades. Those full bodied beautiful queens and princesses of the Mandinka people; my mother was Black, I have 4 Black sisters and countless of beautiful Black Mandinka nieces and nephews, so how can I sit and say that a "Mere White Woman" is better than the loins from whence I come.

And sisters don't think that if you get yourself a White man that you have made it, because you haven't. You would probably be sitting on a keg of dynamite that will plan your death if you cross him in anyway someday. And as far as the upper White society is concerned, White woman will rarely accept you within their ranks; they hate you as much as the White man hate the Black man. What many Black men don't know and realize is that they are sitting at the very beginning of the horn of plenty; you know as well as I do that the Black woman has always supported her man no matter what the situation was, she nurtured you after the white man cut off your foot to keep you from running away, or after beating you unconscious for looking at a White woman.

She bathed and tended your wounds; when you didn't have a job (and still don't) she kept you fed and clothed, when you were put in jail, she bailed your miserable ass out, when your nose was snotty she cleaned it, when you got ill she stayed up with you all night and held you in her loving full bosom where you felt safe and secure, gave you money when you were begging and she tolerated all of your bull s..t. And now you want to say that she is angry, she's a gold digger, but you would never say that about Becky. Becky's are gold diggers too. That is why they are after those NBA and NFL or whatever players, entertainers or actors that they can get. They want the status and the money as well; but Mandingos are not smart enough to see that, they only see that White skin.

Undercover Becky wait right good until his mama has spent all of her money sending him through college, or his Black wife put her career on hold for him, them he becomes a major pick or whatever, then BAM! Becky throws that possum on him and subdue him in a way that he says, Awww Shhittt, mama didn't tell me about this, and that Mandingo nigger is hooked. So at the first sniff of some White ku... he becomes that dog that he always was, but had been in the closet. Becky knows that he will take the bait, and that is why they're sitting just waiting to jump on almost any Black football, basketball, baseball or whatever player that they can. So now he's hooked up with Becky, next comes the divorce and he does not give a damn about Sapphire anymore. And as soon as his Black wife that has supported him throughout his career ask him for money to help support HIS kids, he calls a gold digger. But instead goes right out and send Jacob the Jeweller to his White Becky's house with a suitcase full of diamonds and tells her to pick one. Once the marriage is over, he never visits his children that he has with his Black wife but gets angry when she asks for money for them, and I think that it's a damn shame that a Black woman who has born your children have to ask your new White wife, to ask you for money for your kids. Now this is enough to p... any woman off. And all you Mandingo niggers out there who fit the description I am officially accusing you of treason in the first degree, you have more than anyone else helped to destroy your relationship between you and your woman. Sorry bro-but you can't treat your woman like that without any serious repercussions, that is why many of them are now dating White men.

Angry Black Women

Black woman are the most beautiful woman in the world and the center of what all Black men are about. To deny this is to deny one self and to deny one self is self destructive. So what does the brother do? He tries to justify his insecurities by proclaiming that the Black woman is angry and a gold diggers and this is the major reason why they prefer White women. Yes Black women are angry, and there is nothing more beautiful than an angry Black woman as long as she don't start throwing things. But on the other hand this is typical of that Mandingo back stabbing mentality that was handed down to us from the 13th century.

Sapphire has a right to be angry; especially since she has nurtured and protected your AZ from that very thing that you feel so passionate about, a White woman. Black women know how White women are and Black men are too damn ignorant to realize that his woman is the only one that will protect him. Becky will not protect you, if anything she will call the cops on you. It happens every time; Tiger Woods can tell you this; and look at all the money that his Becky got, serves his Black AZ right. Black women are angry because they have taken care of your butt ever since Dinosaurs have been extinct. And now you have the nerve and the audacity to say negative and derogatory things about her just because she is tired of your SB. And when she start making more demands on you to get your s..t together, you try and turn the table by proclaiming that Black women are "ANGRY". Yes they are and it's because of you, your insecurities, and shallow mindedness.

Black men are saying that they are tired of the Black woman's drama; but Black women are also tired of the drama that they get from the Black man and then decide "enough is enough, there has to be something better". Some sisters would say, don't think that you (Black men) are making us worry about White women taking our Black men. I say good riddance and move on. It is clear that in many cases our men do not value their women or the womb that they came. The chronic amnesia that possesses many Black men's minds in America today is a condition that shows how disturbed Black men really are... Post traumatic slave syndrome, chalked up as colourless love-any excuse will do as long as self Black hatred continues. Stable Black women don't feel the need to have to deal with emotionally unstable Black men with inferiority complexes. When Black men don't love themselves enough to self preserve, the end result will be the demise of the entire Black race in America.

Yes Black woman are angry because they are just tired of the BS, tired of way too many Mandingos, White men and White women are referring to them as "Angry Black Women". Mandingo, this is a phrase that you coined. Yes they are tired of the BS-I repeat, BS that certain Black men say about their mothers, daughters and sisters, the womb of mankind. Sapphire, Sister Girl, Ho, Bitch, whatever you want to call them, proud beautiful and intelligent Black women do not have "lower their standards" in order to compete for a few bad crab apples. I've said this before and I will say it again; the Black woman is the most beautiful woman on this planet, and that's a fact, all you have to do is just open your eyes and you will see... Not only all the beautiful sisters in America but Black women all over the world, in Africa, India, Pakistan, South America, Indonesia, Bahamas, you name it, and what do White folks have Europe, USA, Australia...

As far as beauty is concerned White women don't stand a chance; of course there are also many beautiful White women this is true, but they will never be as beautiful as Black women and they know this; that is why they stay in the sun all day long, trying to get our colour, they have butt fat injected into their lips to try and get those gorgeous sister girl lips, they have butt implants to try and get that sister girl ass that I just love so much. The strength of almost all Black women is magical, contagious, and sometimes frightening because some of them sister girls will knock you out; but Sapphire just as you want Mandingo to respect you, you have to respect him as well, how do you think it looks when Black women are all up in Mandingos face acting just as brutal as he is and always wanting to fight him, this does not make sense to me, because you probably can't beat him anyway-but you are still in his face; so Bobby be careful... The Black woman exuberates just as the Black male majestic power. But on the other hand, you will hardly ever see a White woman being aggressive in this manner to a White man, but she will do it to Mandingo, because he has fallen to the deepest level that he possibly can and this is what she prey on. Some sisters contend that Bobby will treat her better and is a better provider. In many cases this is true but not all cases, I would say about 50% because I know enough White men who are not worth a damn in the first place. Bobby is a better provider because his daddy gives him the better jobs. I know of many cases where Black American woman are totally controlled by her White Bobby, they make no decisions and sometimes don't have access to his bank account. And I also know of other cases where Sapphire has to come out of her bitch bag to let him know that he can't control her. I know of enough cases where Bobby is more than aggressive to his Mandinka woman, threatens her and pushes her around. And as I said sisters, don't think that just because you are with or married to a White man that you have made it because you haven't, they will still call you nigger if they are angry with you; and if you don't believe me, ask Holly Berry. Things like this only show how racist most Whites really are because if you love someone, then you don't throw racist slurs at them.

Once Sapphire gets it in her mind and decide to try out something new, they will eventually look for a White man, just as on Desperate Housewives when Jennifer decides to get with someone else, the first thing that she did was to consider a White man, and as always for the wrong reason. Now this woman to my knowledge was picked up from school daily in a Porsche by her dad, of course she was in a bad relationship with her Mandingo husband, but I don't think that she has had that many bad run ins with Black men. So the first thing that she did was to try and get with this Bobby; now even Ray Charles could have seen that this guy that she was considering getting with was a true gangster, dishonest to the core and murderer, end of story... But I just wanted to relate to you how some Black woman, even though they don't really have a reason, just want to be with or experience being with a White man. And that is ok, but do it for the right reason.

I know many Mandingorettes that are married to Bobby and their life is miserable, and many of the Bobby's have poor jobs and can't provide for their families as they would like to. Even though they are White the educational level is low which equates to a low paying job. But Mandingos be careful because more and more White men are getting with Black women because they love the colour and their strength. But there is one thing that sort of puzzles me, and that is why do many Black women who have girlfriends that are with Caucasian men, will almost never confront their girlfriend about it? Some seem to enjoy the fact that they would be bold enough to do that. But they will always get on Mandingos back for being with Becky. If you walk down the street with a Becky, sisters will look at you like you just killed your mama; but some Black men are no better because they do the same thing. So all of you sisters out there that have problems and issues with Black men dating White women, then you should also have problems and issues with your girlfriend dating White men. That is a pure case of total dishonesty about the situation. These sisters should try and be more honest, if you don't like the brothers doing it you then you shouldn't like it when your girl friend or other sisters do it, and sisters use the same flimsy excuse or reason why they prefer dating Bobby as the Mandingo does about dating Becky.

But Black women please explain something to me because I just don't understand it. Because often times many Black women don't know when they have a good man. And I have known cases where Black women divorced their men because of stupid reasons that are totally ridiculous, and difficult for me to believe, even though I know that it is true; things like "he only wants to sit at home and watch TV"-you see this is really a stupid reason for me because the question is, "what do you want"? Do you want a man that's always running the streets and not caring about you or your children? I ask again what do you want? If your husband or man is at home with you and the children, what do you want? If he is there providing for you and the kids, what in hell do you want? It doesn't matter if he wants too watch television, fact remains that he is at home and that is where he is suppose to be; what you should do is go out and buy him a new TV.

Have you ever considered the fact that the problem might be you? What are you doing to make your husband pay attention to you? Maybe you think just like many other women think, and that is once you get married, and got your man that you don't have to make yourself attractive for him anymore. Are YOU also trying to make the situation better? Don't be argumentative. Have you asked yourself why does he do this? It could be because of you, and if that is the case, girl make yourself sexy, and give that Mandingo a reason to turn the dang television off, and I'm sure that you will see a change.

But one thing is for sure, and that is, when you see Black women fighting like cats and dogs on the internet, no wonder that some Mandingos are turned off. But this you can take to the bank, and that is; if Mandingo keeps going the way he is with all the B-O-B violence and homicides, sisters will not have to worry about being referred to as "Angry Black Women" because there will not be any Mandingos around to make such accusations, because most of them will be in jail, dead or just plain non-existent. African Americans are plagued with a deadly "disease" of brutality, I say disease because it is truly sickening to see what we are doing to ourselves; but the killing part is that most don't seem to care.

Note:
For more information about Black women in the Bible please contact-Daughters Of The Sun- The Bible's Black woman in Prospective by Constance Ridgeway Ph.D. P.O. Box 1132 North Highlands Calif. 95660.

Chapter VI
The White Anglo
Saxon Arian Male

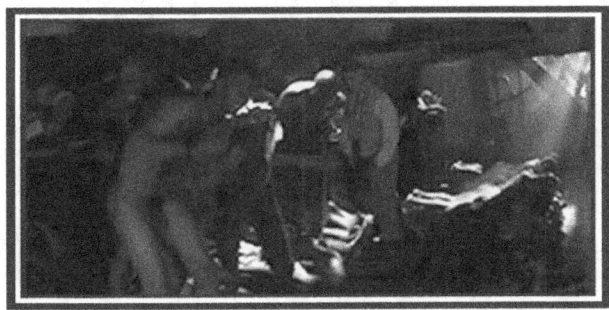

The White man has always felt that he could at anytime he pleased, approach a Black man and ask if he knew where he could get some Black P...y. On the other hand, most White men liberal or racist, can't stand the thought and shock of a Black man being with a White woman. But the White man has always wanted to mate with the savage beast. And at the same time contended that the only thing that a Black man wanted was to screw his sister and that the Black man is possessed with wanting his sister. Well that is only part of the truth-truth is that the White man has always wanted, desired and took the Black woman as he wanted, and the White woman or Black man could not do anything about it. He has always contended that all the Black man wanted to do was be with a White woman, but the truth of the matter is that the White man (this include Jews) has always lusted for and took the Black woman at will. This is evident in all the mulatto babies that were born during slavery times, and don't forget at least 98% of all the plantations in the United States of America were owned by Jews.

And even today I would say that at least 80% of all Blacks living in America have White or Jewish blood running through their veins. White men have always viewed the Black woman's body lewdly and would marvel at her like a dog in heat, her full breasts, big buttocks, legs and everything that made them slaves of the Black woman's sexuality. And in the south White men would even rape Black women in the broad open daylight and nothing would ever be done about it because the Black woman in the south had no rights, not even to her own body. And in former times when a Black woman was arrested in the South she was made to strip in front of the cops, or actually raped. And they did this because they felt that Black women were not human beings, and simply because he could. To him Black women were animals which had nothing to do with God, and he also felt that he could do anything to her without reprisal from the almighty.

You have to give it to them, Black women are arousing to almost all men. They can't help this, it was given to them by God. And during the times of slavery, mulattoes started appearing in the back yards of the Jewish and White plantations in the south. And more and more of these light-skinned mulattoes were running around the yards of the plantation, because the Jewish man as well as the White man was visiting the Black cabins with intense frequency.

The white man may also have thought that his wife was doing as he was, but we all know that it was virtually impossible for White women to slip around with a Black men during slavery times. You see, the White man has this incestuous appetite for Black flesh because he remembers his infant days, and he still has memories of his Black mammy nursing him on her full Black sweet breasts. So he naturally wants to mate with a Black woman; a mother figure, the maid, or whatever Black woman that he can stick his prickly Phallus into. Everything that goes wrong I can blame on the nigger- and I can lynch him for the crimes that I commit against the community, myself, my wife, family, and my feelings and inadequacies. And because the White man has built up such an enormous sexual fantasy and appetite for Black women the mere presence of a Mandinka woman is enough to serve as a sex stimulant and aphrodisiac for many White men.

We All Know What Roles The Jews and the White Man Played In The North Atlantic Slave Trade

But did you also know that, Native American Indians and free Africans also owned slaves?? But the question for me pertaining to the Black slave owners is; were the slave owners Mandinka and were the slaves that they owned from other tribes or from their own people?? I would say that with all possibility, the slave owners were African Mandinka just as the slaves that they owned because as we all know the slaves that were shipped out of Africa were Mandinka people, not all of them but at least 90% of them. So my question is why were they working side by side with the white man in America during the 1800's when they knew that their brothers and sisters were being tormented, dismembered and killed? Were they working to help appease the White man? I would say probably... Things like these that Mandingos do only help substantiate my beliefs, and help to prove my theory even more, because in the case of the African slave owners, it didn't seem to matter if they were Mandinka or other Africans that got caught and kidnapped. It's that special dark Mandinka mentality that causes Blacks to act as they do that is so overwhelming and the many problems that are plaguing African-American relationships today go much deeper than just brothers saying stupid things about Black women on the internet. The current state of the average Mandingo African-American relationship has been carefully planned and designed many years ago. Even if Willie Lynch had anything to do with it or not, fact still remains that the letter hit the nail on the head…Let's say that it wasn't intentional, Black on Black warfare in America is very real.

Blacks still fight each other and the White man still pits us against each other. And since we are apt to turn on each other so easily, explain to me the controversy between the African American woman and man. Black women and children had to watch in fear and shame while Jewish and White oppressors tortured and tormented the Mandingo male into submission to destroy not only his image but the person himself. I don't know how much of this theory of Willie Lynch and his famous letter is true, and I've read many articles disproving that the letter or Willie Lynch even existed at that time. But I do know one thing, and that is the description of the treatments which are describes in the letter were definitely created with these thoughts in mind; because if you look at what has happen to us over the many years you will see a remarkable resemblance to the things that Black men had to endure when the letter was allegedly written.

White Male Sadistic Brutality

Personally my opinion is that White people, and especially White men enjoy killing. And since they considered the Black man worthless and sub-human, this was the perfect excuse for him to murder and torture African people. White and Jewish slave owners used distrust, fear and envy to control the Mandinka people. You know this is true… Because Africans and many Afro-Americans are first of all, very, very superstitious which will always equate into distrust. The combination of the slave overseer treachery, and the overall mentality of Mandinka people in general, was the perfect combination for racist Whites and Jews to control Blacks the way they did; and in many cases instead of the niggers trying to get it together, they were snitching and telling on each other. Remember the slave owners went looking for people that submitted easily and with this natural distrust that many of us harbour for each other, it was the perfect combination for our oppressors to achieve what they did. And this is the exact type behaviour that is basically destroying the African- American community in America today.

The submissive behaviour of Mandinka people, the mental and physical rape of the negro woman and the total destruction of the "Image" of the negro man is in fact that which has happened to us. And we all know the stories that White Americans especially White men, have said about Blacks in general, but the most horrific was to say that Blacks have "Tails", and believe it or not many Whites actually believed this BS. The White racist pigs have always known that there was a surplus of niggers and that is why they have always tried to eradicate us.

They feel threatened for some stupid reason or another I don't know why, as I have said, Black people have never done anything to White people at all. And as far as history is concerned, the Black male or female has never done anything to hurt or control the Caucasian man or woman-but most Caucasians people harbour this hatred because they have been taught to. I'll bet you $10,000 that if you ask a racist white man or almost any White man, if a Black man has ever harmed him physically in any way what so ever-without due cause, the answer will be no; that is if they are truthful.

Almost always they hate Blacks and other minorities because of their teachings from childhood and throughout adolescence; and after adolescence, the ball continue to roll by itself, meaning they teach their children to hate just as their fathers and mothers taught them. Never stopping to think and ask has any Black person done anything to harm me physically or in any way at all? No, but you still hate. Why? Because it's in your blood and nature and many White men have a degenerative, destructive and chauvinistic mindset; he wants to control all, and that's almost all White men; they are working together to help destroy the Black mans image- Germans, Brits, White Americans, Finns-90% of the time, Almost 100% of every damn White person in the world will discriminate against you just because you are Black. Believe me, I have been around the block a few times, and I know what I am talking about; don't forget, I am a Black man too. But I can honestly say that many White people that I know are truly honest and would agree with most of what I am saying, we are all friends because not all White people are racist. And believe me White people have done just as much for me (if not more) in my lifetime than any Black person has; except my father... Let's be clear about this. But in the past even up until today, White people have been giving Blacks a hard time; but it's a new day now! And things have turned and gotten to the point that White males are seriously looking at Black women. Why? Because they find them beautiful, that's why, and believe me most of the time, if a White man is with a Black woman especially in America, and he has a good job and position, that sister on his side will be kicking and I don't blame him, he's trying to get the best that he possibly can get, Black or White, and sisters are the best.

Usually a White man that has a good job will not date or marry the "average" Black woman, and rightly so, I wouldn't have an "average" White woman either, that is if I was interested in one-which is not the case. But anyway the White man has to protect his career, and he can't do this with one of them head shaking Mandingorettes on his side. So if he is interested he will choose carefully and look for the most beautiful and intelligent Black woman that he can find, simply because, he don't want to have to be explaining Nothing??

But sisters be careful of White men they will plan your death in a heart beat, kill you, and be out helping the authorities look for your body. Mandingo will kill you too, but they don't plan it.

And White men will never say bad or degrading thing about their women or their race even when they are with a Black woman. This is only that Mandinka mentality that we all have that causes us to do that. But I would say that the most harm done to mankind has been done by the White man. Because as we all know it's a pattern that has been implemented around the world. They went to these countries bearing weapons of destruction that the indigenous people did not have and started a campaign of mass killing to take control of the people and their country.

Decadents such as Karl Peters which was a racist German white supremacist controlling most of East Africa who held niggers captive in their own country during the 1800s. A brutal and scruple less German Nazi who forced Africans (at gun point) in their own country to act against their brothers to make them submit to his brutal wishes whether sexual or just to kill a nigger or two. Dr. Karl Peters- known as *"Mikono wa Damu"* the Man with Blood on his Hands. Peters was such a decadent and racist that he had his own half white children killed. All in the name of the German government and Kaiser (king) Wilhelm II. And the only thing that the African men could do was to just looked on, because he had the whole German army and government backing him in his murderous adventures. But the natives were helpless, not even their strongest JUJU could help them and of course many of them were afraid of the blue eyed devil... They were afraid of the man with blood on his hands...

With the support of the German government, Peters captured and killed many different types of Africans such as, Herero, Nama, Bushmen and other neighbouring tribes, and exhibited the severed heads, and skulls of these African people in exhibitions all over Germany and the German population went to view those people with the same mentality that they had during the time of the Nazi reign and never gave a damn about the fact that those human beings had been murdered and put in a "Schau Fenster" like mummified animals. They also exhibited cut head where they had been "scientifically" experimenting on the effects of such traumatic injuries to human beings, and of course at that time there were thousands of Dr. Frankenstein's in Germany so they didn't give a crap about no niggers. And that is one of the reasons that Adolf Hitler could convince the German population to act against the Jewish people the way they did, and we all know what happen during the Dritte Reich (3rd Reich). The Germans had already been practicing in South-East Africa long before that, and the methods that the decadents used and implemented to control the Blacks there were extremely brutal and inhumane, and of course Adolf Hitler made Peters a national German hero. Even up to today German parents still keep that racist s..t going by teaching their children to be afraid of Black people.

"Wer hat Angst für (fuer) Schwarzen Mann?
Who's afraid of the Black man?"
"Der Schwarze Mann kommt dich holen!
The Black man is coming to get you…"

These are phrases that many German parents use to control or try to control their children by telling them that the Black man is coming to get them and take them away because of something that they are doing wrong or the parent doesn't like. So they become naturally afraid of Black people. And this is obvious in the way that some German children act when they see Black people. I can remember real good when I was in the military 1970-72 and would walk down the street in Germany and I would walk pass Germans on the way. And after I had passed them a few paces I would turn around only to see that those people had actually stopped, turned around and was watching me like they had never seen a "Neger" (German word for Nigger) before. They would point and say "Kuck mal-der

Neger" look the Nigger... This is racism that is purposely embedded in many German children minds and it is only because their parents use the Black Man as a scaring device to control them at the expense of them being racist towards Black people. The Anglo Sachsen Germans were in Africa just as brutal and full of hatred as their American counterparts were with the Native Americans and Blacks in America. You see that all over the world, South America or in Australia, where White people physically took the land from the Indigenous people living in those countries. And we all know that Whites killed not only most of the indigenous inhabitants in America but their source of energy as well, meaning food. Millions of Buffalo were killed to try and starve out the Indians, not to mention all the other animals that they killed such as wolves, pumas, bears and fox for the European fur market.

Or when Shake Zulu unknowingly allowed hostile British forces to enter Kwa Zulu Natal homelands and we know what happen after that. They have always wanted to own and possess that what we possess including our women, and when I think about Karl Peters in "Deutsch Süd-Ost Africka", I just want to kill f.....s like him. White people never think that they are accountable for atrocities that they commit against other peoples. Only recently in October 2011 the German Government decided after a delegation from the Namibian government raised the issue with Berlin three years ago, demanding that the German government give back the damaged skulls of some 150 Namibian men women and children discovered in medical archive exhibits, to the Namibian delegation in Berlin. Namibian tribal leaders have visited Berlin to collect the skulls of 20 compatriots who died under Germany's colonial rule in the early 1900s. German doctors and scientists had taken the human heads to perform experiments on them trying to prove the racial superiority of White Arian Europeans over Black Africans. In the 1880s,

Germany invaded and took what is now present day Namibia, calling it (Deutsch Süd-Ost Afrika) German South-East Africa, and the earliest attempted genocide in the 20th Century was carried out in 1904 against the Herero people which was the largest of about 200 ethnic groups. The Herero rose up against German colonial rule killing more than 120 German civilians. Of course the German response was barbaric and ruthless. German nationalist and Nazi General Lothar von Trotha then signed a notorious extermination order against the Herero, defeated them in battle and drove them into the desert, where most died of thirst. Only 15,000 Herero, survived from an estimated 65,000 driven from their homelands. Some of the dead had their heads removed and of these, about 300 were taken to Germany, arriving between 1909 and 1914. According to Charite hospital spokeswoman Claudia Peter, " the purported research on the skulls performed by German scientists had been rooted in perverse racial theories that later planted the seeds for the Nazis' genocidal ideology". What the Germans did to those people in the name of their government was wrong. The men were killed by brutal German soldiers while resisting German rule in their homeland. The skulls were stripped of the skin and soft tissue using boiling water and glass shards. They were then shipped to Germany for scientists to test their racial theories. Many were killed in battle, many more died of hunger and thirst after being driven into the desert, or died in concentration camps as a result of forced labour and disease after being taken prisoner. Germany has consistently refused to pay reparations to its former colony, arguing that it has given much development aid to Namibia. But this is a weak argument because the German government paid reparations to the Jews and are still financially supporting the Israeli government.

But even today just as back then, the White man is still practicing genocide but in another way which is to whiten up the Black race in a more subtle way, and are doing with it White women. Becky is infiltrating every aspect of Black society, the music, dance, comedy, you name it. But his plan is backfiring on him, because every time a White woman has a child from a Black man, that child will be Black; and every time a Black woman has a child from a White man, that child will also be Black. So instead of a whitening of the Black race you have a Blackening of the White race. Of course the White man has realized this, and this is why they have to stop niggers another way and that is through the court system and spreading untruths about Black people. But the killing part about it is that the Black man is helping him do it. We all know that the White man does not like niggers being successful, because they are afraid that we would be better achievers than them, that is why they have tried to keep us down all these years-it stand to reason that if a person has nothing to offer but destructive things then, that is what he will do, and how he will be.

White Crime

The FBI collects crime reports from local police, but they are only required to collect reports of murder or homicide. And much of the data and statistics collected should be viewed with more caution because of the circumstances under which the information is being recorded and reported. The American government has always deceived it's citizens, even directly after the 2nd world war our government hired Nazi war time criminals as spy agents when they should have arresting and prosecuting them. So now that we know that, do you think that they will not lie about Black crime statistics? Neither White people nor Black people are angels... White crime is and always has been on the rise and there are statistics proving this. And by the American government not prosecuting many of the White offenders, it has of course created a new generation of White career criminals, because most of them think that they will not be severely punished for their crimes and the White media is already reporting crime associated with Blacks. Even Wikipedia and Google are being evasive about White crime and White crime statistics; they hardly show any of the real statistics because the White media is concentrating on Black people and white crime reports are vague. And if you Google "White Crime" for instance you will get in the results, websites reporting Black on White crime, Black-on-Black, and "White Collar Crime"; and as far as I have seen there are maybe 2 websites on the entire internet which confront and report on White crime stats. White people are not concerned with the crime that they themselves commit but only the amount of crime which Blacks and other races are committing. The principles of justice and equality were and are only words in America, and if you compare how many people that get killed by serial killers, and white kids that have gone crazy you will get a different picture of the overall crime situation in America. The Underwear Bomber, Timothy McVeigh, White mother kills children and blame Blacks, she just drove them in the river and let them drown. And of course the White man will never admit that he is the biggest advocate of violence in America and the entire world, and it all began when they started sending missionaries throughout the world to conquer the indigenous people there.

The media is trying to convince people that violence among White people is next to none. So let us not forget that the typical profile of a serial killer is a Caucasian male. A statistic report on homicide from the US department of justice reports that between 1974 and 2004, of the crimes surveyed that 52% of the offenders were Black and 45.8% were White and 2% were other races. And the victims in those same crimes 50.9% were White 46.9% were Black and 2.1% were other races. According to statistics 84% of all serial killers are Caucasian, and 16% are Black. From slavery up till 2011 White people would kill Black people and it would hardly ever be recorded, but as soon as a Black person does something to a White person, it's all over the news... I'm not saying that Blacks don't commit violent crimes, the only thing that I am trying to show is that White people are doing their share as well and getting away with it. The white media will always sweep it under the rug because they don't want people to really know the truth about White criminals, and the question for me is, what make them think that they are so good when they destroy the whole world with their hatred and aggression?

Never forget now, that Blacks did not create the phenomenon of "Hate Crime" White people started it when they created the KKK (Ku Klux Klan), the Hells Angels, The American Nazi Party, and many other White hate and supremacy groups. These groups have been distributing their hate practices all over America against Blacks since the emancipation of the slave, and the white establishment has done absolutely nothing about it. And now the s..t has turned on them because niggers got tired of Whites killing and lynching Black people while the local police and the American government did nothing about it, except stand by and look on. All of these groups are allowed to exist, but they totally wiped out the Black Panther Party. We are tired of all the racist hatred that was and still is being perpetrated against us by racist White degenerate pigs, we are tired of getting blamed for everything that happens because you're always trying to say that Black people are angry and killing White people, but the point is, that White people have always killed Blacks and have always gotten away with it; but they will never admit this.

If you analyze the American statistic reports that are presented to us by the NSVB and the UCB you will notice that the crime rate for Whites are twice as low as that for Blacks, but the problem here is the fact that the people reporting and providing the statistics, the FBI etc. all make a difference between White and Caucasian-and the classification for

Caucasian include races such as Jews, Russians, Italians, Spanish, Greek etc.. They officially use the word to suggest that the offenders are "not white", and other groups such as Irish, Brits, French, Germans all fall into the classification of White.

Here are some headlines that you hear from Whites but seldom from Blacks:

"White kids arm themselves to the heels with assault rifles, pistols, and shot guns in order to kill at Columbine".

"Fat Nick Gets 15 Years for Bat Attack"

"Nicholas Minucci (Italian name)- <u>Caucasinan</u> American fractured the skull of an African America named Glenn More with a baseball bat and robbed him in June 2005". According to witnesses Minucci repeatedly used racial slurs before and during the attack. A New York Queens jury convicted Minucci of second degree of assault and a hate crime was sentenced to 15 years in prison. Only 15 years?? If it had been a Black man he would have been charged with first degree murder and sent to life in prison.

"12 year old <u>Caucasian</u> boy murders his parents, shot and stabbed his siblings to death because he didn't wand to do his chores".

"<u>Caucasian</u> criminal of the day: Michael Gargiuio responsible for up to 10 murders".

"In 2000 Christine Reed killed her 2 children"

"Christine Yates killed her 5 children because she thought she was a bad mother"

"Jew Josh Cohen stomps 11 month old baby, shook her and threw her out of the bed"

Black people especially Black men have a bad reputation all over the world, but this also includes Black teens as well. Black men for their violence, to each other and Black women for their strength, their assertive, bitchyness or whatever you want to call it, and it does not look good neither for the Black man or the

Black woman as far as the eyes of other people are concerned. It's a sad thing and something has to be done about it. So what are you going to do?? The media and all those racist white oriented websites on the internet are trying to say that white crime is non existent; this is a mass conspiracy and the biggest lie trying to convince people that white violence is next to none and they are trying to keep people from knowing the real truth about White crime.

And the conspiracy of silence is ruining the Blacks in America. Many crimes that are committed go unreported, especially white crime, and there is much more violent white crime committed than many people think there is, because if the American government would require that all felony cases be reported, you would definitely see an enormous rise in White crime statistics. Even though White Americans constitute a vast majority of arrests made they usually go free because of a bias judiciary system against Blacks and other minorities, and as we all know African American are usually poorly represented in our court system.

But the biggest threat to America is "White Power USA". White supremacy groups are increasing exponentially and are responsible for much of the rise in white supremacy violence against minorities in America. White power USA is on the rise and the government is very aware of it-and according to Bob McIntyre, retired special agent and undercover officer for the FBI's federal weapons control agency who states that, "The economy, the Black president, and the democratic controlled congress are things which are fuelling the fire and are factors contributing to the rise in white supremacy violence and hatred in America", and that there are many movements that could spark racial violence at any minute. "The potential and history of violence from white power groups in America is larger than the government wants to admit". There are many splinter white supremacy groups that could spark potential violence at any time and they are recruiting members inside the military, and the federal government. He has hung around all the KLAN rally sites where they complain about the economical and political conditions, and these things are driving the rise in white supremacy violence. Obviously McIntyre is not alone in his concern because last year the US Department of Homeland Security report warned that "right wing extremist groups are the most dangerous domestic terrorist threat to the United States". McIntyre fears that the situation could avert back to the 90s where Oklahoma bomber McVey killed 168 people and that there are many more out there, and Timothy McVey could happen at any day of the week.

Law enforcement around the USA remain vigilant and on guard for the threat that will surely come. From the Hells Angels to the American Tea Party these are the people that are committing crimes against humanity and minorities in America- if not in racist groups then surely as individuals, and that there have been many high profile killings committed by White supremacist in the US since Obamas election and this represent only a small part of the impact that the white supremacy movement has on America. So Black people don't think that we are the only ones who are acting like fools and killing up everybody, because this is definitely not the case, but we still have to get our act together and the things which we are doing under control and not act like our forefathers who bestowed this type behaviour upon us where we kill and destroy each other.

Chapter VII

The White Anglo Saxon Arian Women

It seems that all of our daughters, and our sons have been victimized by the White American sexual nightmare. This nightmare began of course during slavery times when the first light skinned (Mulatto) African-American baby was born from the loins of a Black woman. When the first man was hunted down by a mob of White savage monsters, who ripped off the Black mans genitals for raping a "chaste" White woman, the myth of the sacred and morally pure White woman became reality. Of course this was not created by White women nor sanctioned by Black women. This was of course purely invented by the White man because of his guilt feelings towards the White woman for his persistent and clandestine activities with Black women during slavery. His guilt turned into fear because he probably figured that by him not being able to resist and stay away form the "savage Beast" Black woman, could it be that his woman possessed the same feelings for that "Big Black Savage Buck"? And of course he figured that something had to be done, because the White woman in the south had more or less been de-sexed under the racist indoctrination of slavery. His cohabitation with Black women in my opinion caused him to harbour these feelings of guilt so he puts his woman on a pedestal. She was the "lily pure white goddess", and the most pitiful excuse for the mother of Jesus, because we all know that he has always depicted Jesus and the Disciples in the likeness of himself which is white, because as I have already said, the White man is jealous of what other cultures have and that is why they try to especially hide the "Black Jesus" and the Black woman's presence in the holy bible.

Even if White women married in the south they still referred to her as being "chaste". Even though she had to give up her husband to nasty back yard plantation affairs, many of these women believed that God had ordained that they be deprived of such pleasures and satisfaction. But it became necessary for the White man to portray the Black man as a rapist to satisfy his own guilt feelings. It was also necessary that the White woman accept this image of the Black man as a way of at least proving to herself that she was at least attractive to the savage.

During slavery a few White women rose up and voiced their opinion about the atrocities that were committed against Blacks in their names. Women like Dorothy Tilly who led the struggle against segregation and discrimination. Groups like the <u>Southern Women For The Prevention Of Lynching</u> became active, and these women did everything from fight the KKK to arranging integrated meetings. But all in all the White woman in America was a puppet on a string that did not act against her husbands lust for the Black woman. They would take advantage of the situation and scare or blackmail Black men into having sexual relationships with them, or they would yell "RAPE". And in many White women's minds the Black man is a sexual beast and she feel the need to be protected from him, but at the same time wants and wishes that the Black man touch her. In any case Black seems to be the "Non Plus Ultra" of masculinity and power that the White woman wishes to have. She no longer sees her man in this light. The negro sexuality is also accompanied by other stereotypical ideas that Whites have about Blacks, and White women are definitely envious of Black women; even though they will not admit it, it is the Black woman that is endowed with the physical and sexual characteristics that the White man loves and desire.

But the White man has never ever been alone on his killing rampages; he has always had his accomplices near by. The White man has always put the White women on a pedestal, and on the one hand she is a bit different, but not much; she did not play much of a role in the actual taming of the beast, but she hardly did anything to try and stop it either, especially in the south. But White women really started to show what they were about in the south after the slaves were set free in 1863. From slavery up to present, White woman have always helped in the demise of the Black male, but at the same time she also lusted for that "Big Black Buck", and that's very apparent today.

After the emancipation of the negro, if a White woman had been raped by a White man, they would always look for a nigger that they could hang, the White woman knew that this was not the man that had raped her, but she went along with the hanging anyway; so here it is, the White man has gotten away with the raping of a White woman and the killing of a Black man, and he is still at large to rape her mother, sister, daughter and girlfriend whenever he wished because he knew that "He" would be the one leading the vigilantes to hang the nigger. So this means that the White woman condoned the actions of the White man, and by doing this was contributing to this type behaviour; she was telling him that it was alright for him to commit his sadistic crimes against her, his mother, sister, daughter or any woman he desired to, and it gave him free reign to do whatever he wanted to whenever he wanted to. This practice has continued even up until today where White men are committing a large amounts of crime and are getting away with it, because in many cases White crime does go unreported.

White Female Brutality

When Black men were getting lynched, tarred and feathered, many White women participated if only as an onlooker. Throughout slavery and up to now, white women have been getting niggers killed and hung by the dozens; every time a White woman claimed that a Black man even so much as looked at her, he got his AZ hung, if the poor fool whistled at her he got his AZ hung, if a White man raped her, the nigger got hung. So it didn't matter what happen, the Black male got blamed for every damn thing. Black men should never forget that the White woman has always and always will be on the side of her man and rightly so, and White women and kids were around most of the time when there was a lynching to be done. The Black man has always had to be afraid, especially of White women because he never knew when he would be accused of raping some White woman when in reality a White man had done the raping.

And during the 1960s they were just as bad as their White southern male counterparts; they would call you nigger, spit on you, or did whatever they deemed appropriate at the time. And believe me they helped hang a lot of niggers. But things have changed and those same Becky baby girls that use to get "Negras" hung by the dozens back in the day are now fulfilling that animalistic instinct that they have always had. Many Becky's are trying to and getting to these Big Black Bucks by any means necessary, and at an alarming rate; and in the process helping the Black male to further destroy his own IMAGE, and of course that of the Black woman as well. Mandingo can be, and in many cases is lazy as hell, and most of the time he can depend on miss Becky to support his "lazy by nature" ways. But sister ain't going for that crap any more! Negro you got to get a job... But Becky don't mind because she knows that she can keep him under control and entertained, because he is now fulfilling that animalistic instinct that he has always had, and that is to sleep with a White girl. And sisters have helped her because they have been supporting his butt for all these years and help make him lazier than the law allow. The truth of the matter is that most White women are easy; all you have to do is pat them on the head and you can have sex with them; they don't have the sexual hang ups like Black women have, and this is one of the main reason why many Black man are attracted to them, she will tolerate his BS and keep him down in that dungeon where HE wants to be.

One thing that I noticed is that when a Mandingo gets with a Becky, his whole perception changes and she has totally control over him. He looses his identity! He is on lock down, and if he see a sister he will hardly speak, especially when Becky is with him because he is afraid that she will say or do something to him if he speaks to a Mandinka woman because he is constantly and always under suspicion. Southern White American Anglo Sachsen women have almost always hated the so called, negro man. They are the ones that got you hung back in the day remember? They would have been raped or molested by some White man, but they would always choose a nigger to be lynched. So Black men please tell me-what can you possibly see in the woman that helped so enthusiastically in your demise and what is it that is so fascinating about this woman? Is it the skin color, the hair, the easiness that white women have, or is because she will perform Fallacio on you quicker than a sister will, is that it? Sure it is and we all know that. So let's be real... But don't get me wrong now, I have absolutely nothing against White women; but the truth is the truth. And the things that you like about her are not as strong as the things that sisters are getting on your AZ about-but I think that the most important reason for the Black woman's anger with the Black man is the denial part. And in the event that there is any type of domestic violence she (Becky) will call the cops, they will come with their whips and whip your butt just like they did back then, because they feel that you have no business being with a White woman in the first place, and put your black AZ in jail.

She will call her Mandino "Big Black Buck" a nigger if she is angry with him just as the White man will do if he is angry with his Mandingorette. She will screw your best friend and her brother too. I know that in former times the only thing that the Black man had to idolize was the White woman, and for many years we were forced to see only the White woman's image on the television screen and bill boards all over America. The White women that are successful usually will not date a Mandingo, and if so only a certain type... Because she knows the history as well, and is aware of that sad and sordid story, but also know that not all Black men fall into the same category. But most of the Becky's that are with Mandingos or attracted to them, fit a certain type individual which in most cases is that type of a White woman that a decent White man would not want to be with. Either she is fat and sloppy like a pig or skinny trailer trash. At any rate these are the types that seem to attract certain types of Black men, they seem to prefer trash, and this is the very type that will have him locked up so tight that he couldn't sh.. without asking her.

But since many, many years now White women have found themselves a new source of "LBD". We all know why White women are going to places like Jamaica and the Barbados, or Trinidad and that's only because of the SEX tourism: thousands of American and European Beckys go there wanting and getting that "LBD". This is all they dream about the whole year long until it's time to go on vacation. Once on vacation they go wild, they are typical whores that have jobs in other countries and go to these places to let's say "let their hair down". But it's a trend that we see happening all over the world.

Chapter VIII
American Mandinka Man
Anglo Saxon Arian Woman

Many Black males in America have gone from being a proud Black man during the 1960s to a disgusting decedent of society in 2011. They have gone completely overboard, and they just *"don't make Nigger like they use to..."* The simple fact is that many "Mandingo Men Have Lost Their Minds". Brothers and sisters, Black men have come from the darkest corners of primitive Africa-to being tarred and feathered-to being a sex slave to the White woman.

Can someone please explain it to me? Anyone, because I don't get what the rage is all about. I just don't get it... Especially when there are so many beautiful, intelligent, sweet, loving and dedicated sisters around with dropping it like it's hot bodies, and all the other things that you like, even White men. Is it because you enjoy being lazy and Becky allows you to be like this because it fits her personality and plan as well? Don't get me wrong now; not all White women fit this description, but the majority of White women with Black men fit this description or the reverse opposite, skinny trailer trash that gives you nothing but trouble all the time. And will cheat with you on her boyfriend, your best friend, and cause one of you to get killed.

But before you start thinking that I'm just talking a bunch of crap, I would like to tell you a little story, and reveal a little secret to you. This is only the second time that I am revealing this story because it's really embarrassing, but never the less a true story. And before I start talking about Mandingo or any Becky, I should start with my own experiences with "Weak for Becky" Mandingos.

As I said this is only the second time that I am relating this story, the first time was in 2009 when my sister visited me in Europe and wanted to know why that towards the end of my senior year in college I left town... This is a true story about a Mandinka male and how he allowed his girl friend, which was a White Anglo Sachsen, Italian girl come between us to a deadly point where in order to save HIS life I left town; why? Because I was going to shoot him, simple as that-and by leaving Sacramento I avoided an occurrence which young Black men in America face almost everyday. Don't forget that the #1 killer of Black men are Black men. And this girl actually drove the deepest wedge between two people that could ever be driven.

The scene starts in Sacramento California, where I studied Music Composition which was my major subject area and Business Administration was my minor. In my Junior year at the university, I met in one of my performance classes, a relatively tall dark skinned Mandinka from Florida who was of Cuban descent. We will call him "WEAK", WEAK was also a music student at the university and a real dog for White p...y; WEAK and I hit it off real good, we were both in some kind of a way little gangsters, but that's secondary. So to make a long Story short; WEAK and I
decided to rent a very large 2 story house near the UNI. One of my brothers and another of our classmates also moved in. Everything was going well until the beginning of my senior year in school, when WEAK decided to let his girlfriend move in with him without first discussing it with the rest of us. WEAKs girlfriend was of Italian descent, very tall with long skinny legs, blond hair and no shape; we'll call her "STRONG" and the most disgusting excuse for a White woman that I have ever seen.

Alright, so we tolerated it; that was until STRONG decided that she would rather be with one of the other guys living in the house including myself, than with WEAK. WEAK didn't know that his Becky was hitting on all the guys in the house, truly disgusting. So STRONG Becky couldn't get any play with the guys because first of all, I would never try to screw any of my friends women, I'm not that kind of guy, and I think that the other guys were that way as well. So after STRONG tried but couldn't get to first base with any of us, she decides to put her second plan and tactic into motion, which was to poison WEAK's mind especially against me, because I was not going for her BS of trying to get the rest of us out of the house. I remember the exact day it started...

Earlier that day STRONG and I had this big blow out because what they did was to take all of their utensils out of the kitchen, all the silverware, the pots and pans and everything else that was theirs, but at the same time only using ours. WEAK had said some time before that anything that was in the kitchen and household, was everybody's property and that they would use whatever there was in the kitchen and even eat the food as well. Now, you know how Mandingos are when it comes to grub, especially chicken. So this ticked me off because they were using up everything and were not contributing anything to the household. It all began around 10 o'clock in the morning which was a beautiful spring day 1969. (sound like OJ don't it?) I was in the kitchen having breakfast before my classes when STRONG comes in and start bitching about food in the fridge and other crap, and the more I ignored her, the worse it got. Eventually it got so bad that it pissed me the hell off and I called her a "BITCH" and told her to get out my face. Sometime that day I guess she told WEAK what had happen and that evening WEAK had the nerve to burst into my room and asked me "where did I get the nerve calling his Becky a bitch". I remember that I had been painting, I love to paint, so I put down my brush and asked him was he out of his mind GD mind and what had happen to our friendship? I said that since STRONG is here, there has been nothing but trouble; but he didn't want to hear anything that I had to say and started in an aggressive way to enter my room as though he wanted to fight. You see what WEAK didn't know was that I was a crazy Alabama Mandingo who was heavily involved into Marshal Arts at that time, and I wasn't scared of s..t. WEAK was very persistent, he didn't know what he was doing because he got his AZ whipped and on that day and I almost knifed him because I wanted to put him out of his misery, because he looked very African and I was thinking about how them b.....s over there deceived their brothers for the White man, and now he's trying to do the same thing to me with this B....; Lord forgive me, because I was not raised like that. But luckily for him, my brother was there; he had come up stairs because of all the noise and commotion. I had gotten this boy in a neck lock, and was getting ready to do a job on him, but luckily my brother prevented me from cutting his damn throat; so after that, WEAK turns on my brother and tries to fight him, my bother is about 6'5" 250 lbs, a Marshal Arts expert, just hit him one time in the temple area on his head, and WEAK loss all sense of reality; he ran down the hall way which was about 30 feet long, went into the room at the end of the hall and tried to jump out of the window form the second floor, he could have gone down the stairs, but at the time his mind was not functioning properly. And the only thing that prevented him from jumping out of the window was our roommate at the end of the hall.

That was an AZ whipping that, that Mandingo will forever remember, and because of this AZ whipping, he decides to try and harass me; he just didn't know that I was one of them Mobile Alabama Mandingo niggers that grew up picking cotton, plowing the fields, getting my AZ tarred and feathered, torn apart by horses, whipped to near death by the White man, and I grew up fighting everything from Mandingos to wart hogs. Needless to say that WEAK and STROMG got their butts out of there; I don't know where they went but they got out of that house. So what followed was a string of harassment tactics geared towards me. I

was the bad guy and STRONG had nothing to do with all this…
I received threatening phone calls from him, his mother and
brother, saying that they would all get me… Now I'm going to
tell you something that I'm really embarrassed about-but it's
the truth. After all the threats, I did get a little scared until a
Caucasian American friend that had moved in to replace
WEAK and STRONG, we'll call him Joey, offered to sell me a
weapon for $25 because he needed money; this was a 45 calibre
Smith and Western, and could get the butter from the duck.
Joey was also a student at the university. So I purchased the
weapon and was actually packing this gun with me on the
campus of the University and in all my classes. Because WEAK
basically knew my schedule, what he would do was to squeak
up besides me on the campus parking lot or on the street with
his car and say things such as "I'm going to get you " or "your
AZ is dead" "the cops are looking for you" "my family is
looking for you". This of course went on for quite some time,
until one day he scared me so bad that I pulled out the gun was
getting ready to fire, but he pulled away just in time. Now, is
that not sick??

This is when it hit me and a little voice said Don, get out of
Dodge. So I decided to save my life and his by allowing myself
to be inducted into the military (I could have fought it), getting
as far away from California as I could. So what happen was
while I was contemplating what I was going to do, the draft hit
me again. At this time the Viet Nam war was still raging on, and
I had always beat the draft because of being in school. I could
have stayed in college because I had a Psychologist helping me
stay out of the draft; but because of my situation at the time, I
decided to go into the military, and throughout my military
career, which lasted only

Note: Please don't get me wrong, I am not bragging about my deeds or anything like that, I'm
only relating these things to you to support my statements about White women and how
Mandingos go crazy when they get to sniff a little White p…y…

18 months, I played trumpet in the military band in Frankfurt Germany. This is what saved WEAK'S life, because another month or so and it would have been too late for both of us, especially him.

Divide and conquer, this is a perfect example of how a Becky can poison the mind of a stupid Mandingo and get him to do whatever she wants. He didn't want to hear anything that I had to say, and I found out years later that WEAK actually killed a mutual friend of ours over a $5 bag of weed and was serving a life sentence in Folsom Prison. Again I would like to know what it is that Becky possess that appeals so much to the psyche of Mandingos to cause them to act the way they do when they are with White women? Is it the BS that they are telling you about sisters? Or do they give better head? Now that would be a reason-but sisters give head too... So what is it? Can anyone tell me??...

Because the reasons that are presented to us are not acceptable to me. Reasons such as, "the Black woman is angry" of course she is because she not only have to deal with your BS she has to deal with Becky's as well- "Black women are gold diggers" Becky's are gold diggers too; you are just too stupid to see this- yet and still when a Black woman have your babies, you are not decent or man enough to take care of them, but you will take care of the kids that you conceive with your Becky. A true DEPENDENT Mandingo nigger following the footsteps of his ancestors and planting seeds all over the place.

Status Symbol

Many Mandingos think that by having a White girlfriend or wife that they have "arrived", you are now a status symbol. A white Woman will never boost your status in society, because it's not about the White woman it's about the White man. He makes the decisions and he still thinks that you are that same "COON" that he use to hang from the tallest sycamore tree back in the day. And believe me brothers and sisters we are still sitting at the bottom of the totem pole, but most of us are too stupid to see and realize this. Now days many Mandingos are primarily concerned with getting themselves a Becky, but the question for me is why do you have to change your personality once you get with a White woman? Our hero Frederick Douglas was married to a white woman; goes back a long way doesn't it? But he also knew which side his bread browned on. All you Mandingos out there claiming that you like White woman because Black woman have driven you to them is the biggest Mandingo lie that I have ever heard. Just go on and admit that you want and like that white skin, and don't try to blame others for your insecurities, because Mandingos seem to become pu....s when they get themselves a Becky.

Case scenario: I know this Mandingo that is lives in Europe and is married to a German Becky. She has him so wrapped up that he don't know up from down not to mention who he is. His Becky travel to the Bahamas or Dom Rep. once or twice a year explicitly to visit her lover, and the crazy part is that her Mandingo knows about her escapades of love and that poor bastard can't do anything about it... Why? Because he is living with her in her mothers apartment, and is basically living on her expense account; this is the way she keeps total control over her Mandingo; and I will bet you a dollar against a hole in the wall that he would not take this from a Black woman. He is a perfect example of that type Mandingo that I have been referring to and he does not want Becky to put his AZ out, so he tolerate her BS which also include bad mouthing sisters. He is obviously too weak of a man to tell that b.... where to go. This is a typical case where a Black man, with a White woman that is too weak to stand up for himself and being totally controlled by her. But when I really think about it, this Mandingo falls into that very same category that many Mandingos fall into when they are with

Becky women which includes low intelligence and self esteem, very low educational standard, lazy, undependable, you name it. So you can see how and why such men allow themselves to be bluffed, dominated and controlled by White women. No matter where they are Black men act like they are scared to speak to a Black woman if he is with a Becky... Brothers it's disgraceful but if you really think about it, many Black men are giving up everything that they have; you've not only casted your woman aside but also that little pride that you yourself had.

Remember when James Brown said "say it loud I'm Black and I'm proud"? And Black men weren't being so stupid? When the Black Panther movement gave Black women and men a sense of pride in the fact that they were Black people, proud people from Africa, so what happen to that big strong Black Mandingo nigger that the White man was and still is afraid of? But as I said Black males do not pose any type of threat to White males or females, and we never have. The reason that Black men go to White women has to do with their state of mind. And believe me Black men, your current state of mind has nothing to do with Black women, and it's time for Mandingos to start standing on their own two feet and stop letting women take care of them, whether Mandinka, Anglo Sachsen or otherwise.

But how can this take place especially since the White man has already stripped him of his identity in the first place? The real and conscious Black man in America recognizes the atrocities and the demonic practices which have been bestowed upon him by the Jews and Whites, and has gotten out of the slump without the help of a White woman, but with a sister girl on his side. The majority of Black men in America are sticking by their women, because they value their mothers and their sisters and daughters- they are still loyal to Black women, and don't try to put them down like that very small percentage of Mandingos that try to bad mouth sisters. And these same Mandingos often allow Becky to say racist things about Black women and not step up to the plate and speak up for his woman. But the reason why he has no interest in doing such things is because he is sexually influenced and being enabled by White women. This type Mandingo seems to forget that his mother is or was a Black woman; I know; you're probably thinking that maybe his mother is White; but his daddy is Black, and fact remains that if a person has one tenth African blood in them, then they are niggers, according to the White man that is.

Remember the Mandinka people were put into slavery partly because of their submissiveness. And for me any Black man that say anything negative about our Black women, especially in the presence of White people be it man, woman or child are in my book traders and ignorant about their own race. But these type Mandingos are usually pretty illiterate, have basically no education, don't want to work, fornicate all the time, are dishonest, dubious, and lazy as hell. But one thing is for sure, and that is, you will hardly ever hear a White woman say anything racially negative about a White man. And this also applies to the Caucasian man. Sisters on the other hand do! And that is in both cases that Mandingo mentality at work. But we all know that this applies more to the Black man than it does the Black woman.

Becky has turned these Mandingos into a type of machine that is even worse than when they (we) started out because they (Becky) caters to that "Laziness By Nature" way that is so present in the natural makeup of many Black men. By Becky supporting his clouded mind and psyche the way she does, she is totally controlling his mindset as he becomes more and more dependent on her. This is a typical Black mans relationship with Becky-case scenario-Black guy get involved with a Becky, she already have 2 or3 kids from different Black men and maybe one White man. So this dumb ass Mandingo hooks up and moves in with her in her apartment. Remember now she already has 2 or 3 kids, and probably only 20 years old. She immediately gets pregnant and there he is helping to take care of some else's children, but he probably wont leave his Becky as quick as he would Sapphire. This is a typical case of a Mandingo thinking with the wrong head. Now this lazy bastard is her problem, and Becky is now more than ever ticked off at Black women for allowing her to take his sorry AZ from her in the first place. So what does she do, she bad mouth the Black women.

And what does Mandingo do, he supports her. Another type of Black White relationship would be a Becky that is much older than the young Black buck which is keeping her satisfied 24/7; sexually that is, because we all know that she is supporting him. This is the type that will more than likely call the pigs if he does something that she doesn't like. She is older and have more experience, but still have 2 or 3 "churen" by different men. So in both case scenarios this poor bastard is so much in love with this White tramp that he marries her, she immediately gets pregnant to keep him around, and there he is trapped like the hopeless degenerate pig he is. Now don't get me wrong now, these are case scenarios that I personally know of… But I ask you again, somebody please, please tell me what is it that is so fascinating about a half illiterate poor, skinky sweaty 300 pound Becky that is causing such havoc and confusion in Kinta. Is it something that Kinta is eating? Or is it sometimes that is part of a covert conspiracy to totally disable the Black man through poor lily white trashy woman? This might sound foolish, but who knows? But there is one thing that the slave masters never figured in their plan, which was that his little bitty Bouncing Becky Baby Girl would wind up screwing niggers.

NFL, NBA, Actors-one thing that they all have in common is that they try to say that the Black woman is a gold digger after the break up because she has to ask him for money to help support HIS kids; but they don't say that about Becky, they just pay that 100 million and shut the hell up, don't they Tiger? Black

I KNOW WHY MANINGOS SING

women have always been in their lives, so why does the Black
woman always have to be the gold digger? Why does she always
have to take a back seat? In most cases she does have your
children... Do your own kids mean that little to you? And why
don't you pay child support? Because you are a lazy good for
nothing Mandingo Negra that's why. And believe me, many
Black men prefer White women or light skinned Black women
because they think that their social position will be enhanced
with a Mulatto or White woman. And I can imagine how Black
mothers must feel who's X-husbands were stars like Michael
Jordan for instance who teaches his son the advantages? Of being
with a White woman. You know it's amazing how much these so
called Black man support White people, because every time we
get a little money the first thing that the Black man does with it is
to give it right back to the White man, even if she was a White
woman, some White person will get that money some day.

I think that it is strange, a bunch of crap and a disgrace to
Black people when Mandingos say that they don't like the way
sisters act, but don't you thing that it's a bit strange that when
White women get with Black men, the first thing that they do is
to try to act like sisters? So Mandingo what do you want? And if
a White woman fights him he just run and act like the little punk
he really is; but if a sister does the same thing he would
definitively fight her like he would a man, and be much more
aggressive to his own sister than he would to a White woman.

And I have heard many young Black men in interviews say
that they have been hurt or picked on by Black women and that
is the reason why they go to White girls-now if they keep this up
I'm going to start crying, such flimsy excuses; I mean are they all
punks? But the point here is that Black men will more readily
fight a Black woman than he would a White one. And this is
basically because he is afraid of the retaliation from the White
man. This is typical Mandingo behaviour, instead of trying to
fight the oppressors we fight and kill each other just as we did

101

during the 13th century when the Arabs enslaved Mandinka people with the help of other Mandinka, and it's the same way today. And now, app. 148 years later after being freed, that other part of that Mandingo BS has kicked in, and we are killing and hating each other more than ever. But we all have these type of individuals in our families, that lazy good for nothing Mandingo who would rather take his chances, and get his disability or welfare check than trying to create some type of meaningful and stable situation for themselves and their families. Never forget, White women have always lusted for Black men, they just couldn't show it because of the retaliation from the White man, we can go as far back as Frederick Douglas, 1818-1895 or Jack Johnson 1878-1946 they both had White women during a time when it was totally taboo for a White woman to associate with a Black man, but they eventually found a way, and it has gotten so bad that Mandingos don't know which way to turn.

Chapter IX
American Mandinka Woman
White Anglo Saxon Arian Man

It seems as though Black women have found a way to resolve the problem with the "shortage" of Black men. Black women have begun to expand their options by dating outside of their race. But the reason that there is a shortage of Black men in the first place is because there are, according to statistics app. 1,300,000 more Black women than there are men. Others are gay or on the "Down low", and if a man is on the down low, then he's gay for me; especially if he likes booty. According to the latest stats, the U.S. Census Bureau says that there are around 791,600 Black men incarcerated, and others who have White women. But there was a rise in Black White marriages from 27,000 in 1980 to 80,000 by year 2000. The reason for this increase in more Black women dating White men may be attributed to educational attainments by Black women. A study revealed that the number of Black women earning degrees increased by 55 percent since the mid 70s, but only by 20 percent for Black men, says Nichols Nash, a journalism professor at Arizona State University.

"Women who go to college and graduate want someone with the same educational level or more. But Black men just aren't there, so that could be one reason why more Black women are dating White men. But on the other hand some Black women are just the same as that ignorant Mandingo and try to say things about Black men like I can't stand that nappy hair and stupid crap like that, hell your hair is nappy too or haven't you noticed?

One could write a lot on the subject of black women's flimsy excuses or reasons for dating white men, but the situation is not quite as bad as with Mandingo. And many Black women are not helping the situation either, many of them do the same thing that the Black man does and try to discredit her man; and they say racist things about them just as the Black man says about the Black woman. The Black woman has always been the sexual slave of the Jew and the White man; they consistently and systematically ripped her of her identity as a proud Mandinka woman; even President Thomas Jefferson raped and forced many of his slave "nigger bitches" to submit to his animalistic sexual desires. The Blacks that worked in the house were usually the salve masters offspring's of the slave girl or girls that he had raped and she (they) bore his child or children.

The term Mulatto originates from this period and means a forced bred Mandinka woman that had given birth to a mixed child from a White or Jewish man. Thus the child having hair between Blacks and Whites, other Negroes referred to them as having "good hair". Now this also help set the scene for Black on Black racism, because the half Whites in the house thought that they were better than the niggers out in the field mainly because they stayed in the house with the master and his family because they were his children. We see the separation and this behaviour among ourselves when Black men and women refer to other Blacks as having "good hair" when it's a little straight or curly. Black folks hair is better anyway, because it hardly stinks when you don't wash it, and it might be kinky but it protects your head better from the sun than theirs.

We all know that even during slavery times some Black women willingly married White men, it was not always rape; and the few Black men like Frederick Douglas married White women, but that all depended on where they were, because we all know that Black men were getting hung by the dozens for just looking at a White woman in the south. But as I said before, sisters use the same flimsy excuses why they prefer dating Bobby as Mandingo does about Becky. But sisters you can't complain because the moment many sisters have the chance they also get themselves a Bobby. Some of their excuses are similar to that what the Mandingo male is saying about Becky-the straight hair, the white skin, the blue eyes, you know all that bull that Mandingos males and females like and are saying about why they like Bobby and Becky. They never have reasons like, she's smart, or he's a decent person, nothing like that. And why do sisters always say that their girl friends Bobby is cute? Child he so cute-bull shit, he ain't that cute, and 90% of the time they will say this, but they will never say this about a Black man. They are just as much an Uncle Toming Mandingorett as this type of Black man is an Uncle Toming Mandingo. This is the way I see it...

Beautiful Black women have beautiful Black sons, so why the hell HE got to be so damn cute all the time? He is no better, and he definitely does not look better than any Black man; but Mandingo women would hardly ever say this about the Black man that her girlfriend is dating or married to, to her he is just another "nigger". Almost always it's the hair, skin colour and the blue eyes. And there are a lot of sisters out there that will not under any circumstances be with a Mandingo. She says that Bobby showers her with gifts, well he should, because if she is beautiful he truly has a gem, so he should reward her. But sisters wake up... 99% of the time all White men just want to screw you, try and get the him to marry you and see what happens. Oh yeah they will screw you but try to get him to take you to his mama, this he will almost never do. I have known of many cases where certain sisters that I knew, only had eyes for Bobby, one in particular tried to get her Bobby to marry her but he wouldn't; and there she was pleading like a slave on the ground begging the master not to whip her and acting like a fool for this man to marry her and he wouldn't. Black women often think that a White man is the answer to their dreams and strive to get a White man when they should be striving to get and man that will honour her, Black or White.

But Sapphire don't seem to realize that not all White men are made of the s...t that they and many Black women think they are made of. But many of them are smart though, got to give it to them, as a matter of I will be the first to say that I'm glad they're around because if we had to depend on some of these Mandingos around here nothing would ever get done. But I really can't see for the likes of me why any Black woman in America would want to be with the devil himself; why would she want to be with a person that has and still is consistently causing havoc and despair among Black women and men all over America for over 300 years. That has not only raped your body but your mind as well, he has stolen everything from you, and you are still content with the few grams of bread that he throws your way.

A man that has completely changed your natural way of being. It seems that Black women are totally unaware of this all too important fact about the White man. I personally don't trust most of them, and Black women you have just as many reasons to hate HIM and what he did to you, your mother, sister and daughter as the Black man has. Please don't misunderstand me I'm not advocating hatred; but the truth is the truth and sometimes it might hurt a little. I'm like my Irish friends that I have that would never bow down to the Brits and their control over Ireland, and I will never bow down to the man that so many Mandinka women are starting to look up to so much. For as long as I'm on this planet, he will never change and he will always harbour special hatred and use discriminatory acts against you and me wherever he can. He will throw you a few crumbs, and you will accept them willingly, doing exactly that which HE has taught, trimmed and trained you to do so well for so many years.

Now sisters I ask you honestly, do you really want to be with a man that has taken you and turned you into a complete submissive slave and ruined your all too important family structure then and now? Do you want to be with a person that has deliberately taken your man and son and made a mule out of him? Do you really want to be with the man that has continually beaten and killed Black men for hundreds of years? Is this the man that you want that has systematically changed your natural state of being to fit his sexual and economic desires? If it is, then I wish you luck, for I would think twice before making that decision, but be careful for what you wish for because you just might get it. So when you check it all out, Mandingos and Mandingorettes that date outside of their race almost always say the same thing about each other. And sisters you can't tell me that you don't do this because I have heard it with my own ears many times, and I'm sure that your Bobby has asked you at one point or another, why do you only date White men. So what would your answer be?

Excuse me for repeating myself, but you will hardly ever hear a White man or a White woman saying nasty and degrading thing about their race. This is only that Mandingo mentality that we all have and use to hurt each other with. And in all honesty I truly believe that Black men do much more to hurt Black relations than the Black woman does, especially since we have radio, television and the interne. Of course Mandinka men have always been pitted against each other since slavery times, which was another method that Whites and Jews used to keep us suppressed. They would pit the young male savage against the older male savage, the Mulattos against the darker Blacks. But then at one point we almost got it together and almost rid ourselves of this curse in the 60s. But at that time there was a great divide in the community, because there were 3 major fronts that especially Black men were following. On the one side you had the Black Panther Party, on the other was the Black Muslims movement and of course Dr. Martin Luther King with his racial equality for all Americans through his infamous non-violent movement. And the only thing that the White man could do during the 50s and60s to contain their niggers was to increase the hangings, (because they no longer saw niggers as an economic commodity), police brutality, and the media which was the radio, television and tabloids all participated.

The American government totally eradicated all of the Black Panther Party-kill almost all of them and the ones that are not dead are in exile or have died in jail-I think that Bobby Seal is still alive and Huey was in South Africa but was shot to death in 1989 by Tyrone Robinson in Oakland Calif. But as time progressed, instead of getting better thing got worse because niggers were in an uproar. Could this be the phenomenon that would bring them back together?? So the White man had to find other tools to keep the Mandinka down. But his greatest tool of all was the law. He had the law on his side, and we all know that Blacks get more prison time for the same crime as Whites do. He has always created new methods of harassment and means to keep the Mandinka people under control and with the creation of the media, radio, television, internet, even though it was not the original purpose, it also help keep Blacks under control. But now days Blacks do this themselves, still turning on the axis just as the White slave master predicted. Blacks consciously and subconsciously treat each other the way we do because we have a natural hatred for each other and have been taught to do so throughout the decades by the Jew and the White man.

The radio was not so much threatening to the psyche of the Mandinka as much as the television and the Internet is. And with the television he continued his suppression of the Afro-American woman's natural psychological state by forcing her as well as the negro male to watch only White women on Television all day long- that is if they had a T.V. because back in those days the only women to be seen on a television screen were White women because the Black woman had to endure the stripping of her natural self, and television was just another tool that the White man used to accomplish this. He put White women on the screen so that the Black man would desire her instead of his own woman, and if you saw any Black women on TV they were always servants. That is until shows were created like the Amos and Andy show, but even then Sapphire played the dominant roll, and Kingfish played that conniving stereotypical Black (savage) Mandinkan male image; slick, lazy, greedy, deceitful, stupid, dishonest to the core and always trying to get something for nothing. I really can't see for the likes of me why any Black woman in America would want to be with the devil himself but for that matter I really can't see why a Black man would want to be with the woman that has constantly gotten him lynched for decades. Because she is from the same seed as he, she will not protect you from HIM, don't you get it?? But Sapphire, the only thing that I can say is that if you want to be with the man that has consistently and systematically raped you, your mother your daughter and your sister and changed your natural way of being, then go ahead maybe you deserve each other anyway.

If you want to be with a person that has and is still consistently causing havoc and despair among Black women and men all over America, then you go ahead; a man that has not only raped your body but your mind as well and has taken everything from you, and you are still content with the few rusty pennies and bread crumbs that he throws your way. Black women as well as Black men seem to be totally unaware of this all too important factor about our oppressor, and about our behaviour to each other as well. I wouldn't be with that devil, especially knowing what I know about him and his woman; I'll take my chances with Sapphire. Because the man that so many Black women are looking so much up to will never change and he will always have special hatred and use discriminatory acts against your brother, kill them and put them in jail; he will throw away the key and cause you to moan and groan for your love one, doing exactly that which you have been doing for decades.

Chapter X
Black Entertainment

One of my favourite shows when I was a child was the Amos and Andy show. Sapphire directed her anger at her husband George (King Fish) Stevens, but hers was not the generalized anger that is associated today with the so called angry Black women. Even though I enjoyed those shows when I was a child, they were still racist and displayed Black men in a very distasting manner. During the days of slavery in the United States of America, the African slaves entertained themselves and others with musical and dance forms that contained elements of the forms that they brought with them from Africa. Some of the dances the slaves created went on to become national dance crazes for Black and White Americans alike such as the Cakewalk, and later the Black Bottom; the Charleston and the Lindy Hop which emerged out of Harlem in the late 1920's contained many African characteristics. And if you have ever seen Africans dance then you know why we are the leaders. Africans dance with their whole body. And believe me I have seen some things that 99% of Americans Black or White will never ever see. The Charleston for instance was a series of steps which are thought to have originated with African Americans who were living on a small island near Charleston, South Carolina. And that the steps first originated from the Cape Verde Islands near Western Africa. But others also hold the Ashanti People of West Africa (Ghana) to be the originator of the dance.

When Africans dance there are often time many acrobatic stunts that are performed in the dance, sometime it would be a ritual dance or a tribal or whatever, and as you can see from the dance styles from groups in Bukino Faso or Sierra Leone that we get our dance spirit from West Africa. Mandingos are the best entertainers in the universe, and that goes especially for music, dance and comedy. Tap Dancing, The Jitterbug, Black Bottom, Charleston, Lindy Hop and many more dance steps were created by Mandinka people, and we all know that White folks can't dance. I think that they hear a different beat.

Mandingos are especially good at doing 4 different things; music, song, dance, and talking crap... which by the way also include acting. Oh, yeah! Mandingos know how to talk crap... We have a gift for GAB that is unprecedented in hardly any other race of people which can sometimes be very annoying; and Hip Hop is all about niggers trying to get their rap on.., we use to do it when I was a kid. But in reality, and all kidding aside, Mandinka people do not know their worth. Most of the major modern dance, (pop) music and song directions can be attributed to Mandinka people (except classic). What is it that makes us so successful in the arts? Is it that all too familiar Mandinka "High Life" music and rhythms which are embedded in our souls? You see this all over the world where Mandinka people live, especially in Africa, North America, South America, and the West Indies. We were all transported from our homelands to these parts of the world. Reggae and Maringa music are forms of Highlife music, and 99% of the time, when you hear High Life music you cannot sit still, and with Raggae and Maringa music it's the same thing. Music is a force that we as humans cannot

111

contend with even though we can control it. Whether from Africa, North America, South America, Middle America or the West Indies, Mandingos *"Make The Music That Rock The World!* West African High Life, Raggae, Rag, Big Band, Blues, Gospel, Rock and Roll, Jazz, R&B, Free Jazz, Hip Hop, Funk, you name it, the music that modern whites listen to today was and still is being created by Mandinka people. And Mandingos sing because the music forces us to. We have no choice in the matter, it was given to us by God and no man on earth can take that away from us, especially a White man.

We (Mandinka) sing when we are happy and the Mandinka have special songs for this, just as they have special songs for times when they are sad, and the music forces all of us to do this, we sing because in a work situation it makes the chores easier to accomplish when everybody is moving at the same time; and the most musical people in the whole wide world are the Pygmies; that's right- Pygmies. Why? Because they have a natural "Counter Point" in their music that no westerner can contend with; and Counter Point is considered in the western world as the "Highest" form of musical expression. And whether you know it or not, there are of course many classical music instruments that have their origin in Africa such as the Violin, the Trumpet, Oboe and many more.

Other than Classical and folk music like Country, Hill Billy or German Schlage music, Whites do not have much to offer as far as modern music and dance is concerned, and every time there is a "New Musical or Dance Direction", all the Whites jump on the band wagon. This is very evident in Hip Hop and Rap music; every body wants to be a rapper-remember the 4 things that I said that Blacks could do well? One was talking crap-and that's just what Hip-Hop and Rap music is all about, "Niggers" talking s..t.

Chapter XI
The Media

And speaking of niggers talking crap- I would like to make one thing perfectly clear; those Mandingos that are putting up all these videos, and talking all this BS with their bad English do NOT speak for all Mandingos in the United States of America, let us be perfectly clear on this. The media is helping the Black man to destroy his own image and the image of Black woman and Blacks in general-they want to reverse the order and destroy the image of the Black woman now, her psychological self has already been destroyed, now they are after her image; and they are doing this through the Black man, and the White man already aware of the Black mans weakness, because his father has already told him what they are... White women.

These type pissy punk Mandingos want everything too easy, which fit right in with their Mandingo mentality, schematic and agenda. And this is why Mandingos get themselves a Becky, because they cannot deal with the strength of the Black woman, and Becky is not going to give them too much static because she is just glad to be on board. I think that among all of the media devices, the television and the internet has done more to help with the demise of the Mandinkan image than anything else. Insecure Black women are also doing their part to destroy the Negro males image and also destroying her own state of psychological consciousness at the same time. She is also a victim of the media, and she now has to tell the world what she think about Black males and how disgusting she finds them. But I think that anyone who has the nerve to talk about their own race the way some Mandingos do on the internet or any media form, then it's alright for me to burst them out in a book.

And the media has given way to many diabolical advocates of separatism including many Blacks. In the past it was radio, tabloids, and the television that were the culprit media forms that were helping to keep Blacks under control, but the radio was not as threatening to the psyche of the Black woman. With the television, the White man continued his suppression of the negro woman's natural psychological state by forcing her as well as the negro male to view only White women on television thus making the White woman that lily pure an unadulterated Arian symbol. Because back in those days the only women that could be seen on a TV screen were White women, and the Black woman had to sit and endure the stripping of her natural self. And the White man has always created new methods of harassment to keep the Mandinka people under control and with the creation of the media, radio, television, and the internet, even though it was not the original purpose, it also help keep the Mandinka people in psychological bondage.

Today light complexion Black women like Dianne Carroll, Vanessa Williams, Hally Berry, Vivica A. Fox, Kerry Washington are the type Black women that are preferred by film producers, directors, television and the media; now don't get me wrong now, I have nothing against light skinned Black women, high yellow no yellow, if she is a Black woman then I am automatically on her side. But unfortunately most of the Black women which are presented in the media today are light skinned Black women, even our Black film producers prefer mulatto women over darker skinned Black women, why? Because they are still hung up in the stereotypical image of a "Beautiful Black Woman". Dark skinned women are less desirable, and in most films where the stars of the film is a middle class Black family 90% of the time the husband complexion will always be much darker than his wife's complexion. Even producers such as

114

Spike Lee, whom I truly respect a lot in his film Jungle Fever, the wife was a very high yellow Black woman, but on the other hand you have producers like Tyler Perry who seems to be more aware and conscious of this fact, because he uses in his films brown to dark skinned Black women. Of course our attitude against our own people help perpetuate the bias attitudes and problems facing Black women in the media, be it film or television. Beautiful dark skinned Black women are still being discriminated against in the media, and this make them think that they are unworthy, because they hardly get work, and this is what the White man has always told her and the Black man as well, and often times back in the real world, many Black men are looking for a White woman or a light skinned Mulatto Black woman.

Religion and the Media

Worship and religion in many African American churches have become pure entertainment. Chicken eating preaches, instead of trying to eat all the chicken that those sisters in the church are fattening you up with-maybe you should try to do something good for a change and try and put some programs together that will help give young Black men and women a sense of responsibility and worth. When I go to church it's not about how I look or what I seem to have. It's only about worshiping the Lord and doing the right thing. I notice that most of those chicken eating preachers, the ones who say that they have been called by the holy spirit to spread and preach the Gospel truth have some type of criminal background or some devious things that they were doing to caused them to get incarcerated in the first place, and now have guilt feelings, thus causing them to choose the ministry as a way out of their dilemma. But the question is; how can a person who claims that they have felt the hand of the lord be so money hungry? My Dad didn't allow preachers in the house. Even though my mother was extremely religious he knew then that, that was all just a game and that they only wanted to use people, especially all those lonely sisters in the congregation waiting for their chance to get to the preacher. I can remember when I was a kid, our preacher once told my dad "Brother Payne, you've never invited me to your home", and my dad said "If I don't invite you, don't come". Today preachers like the right reverend Creflo Dollar are helping to keep Black women and men down with the help of the Internet. But what puzzles me is that they can't see the BS surrounding many of these so called "Right Reverend" chicken eating preachers, whose only purpose in life is to beg. I know that not all preachers do this but, far too many of them try and play on the poor and use scare tactics to get then to pay their "Tides" for instance knowing full well that many are on welfare and that little check that they get is hardly enough to pay the bills and buy food. But the right Reverend tells them that the Lord will make a way-this is true especially since the Holy Father has already provided for them to get their welfare check in the first place; so why would a man of God expect a mother on welfare with 3 or 4 children to pay Tides when she can hardly feed her family and pay their bills??

Why would a man of God want to take that money? This is pure greed and the mindset that many Black ministers have in America today. The right Reverend should be trying to help these families rather than ridiculing them in church when they can't pay their Tides, and I've seen this many times. It's just greed that's all that it is. And believe me people, the "Gospel Word" is not and has never been for sale. Black preachers are only steering their flock in the wrong direction away from God and towards the devil, and using scare tactics to control the people in the congregation. But the chicken eating preacher that takes the cake for me was the right Reverend Dr. James David Manning. I must add here that I was surprised to hear that Dr. Manning had passed away on April 1st 2011, which incidentally is April fools day, and we all know that he was the biggest fool in town. I don't want to talk negatively about the dead, but I remember that he would speaks with such contempt and such anger. Don't get me wrong; there are enough Black ministers out there who have studied theology and not necessarily been called to preach by the Holy Spirit. Now I don't want to say anything bad about anybody but we must see the truth for what it is.

Ministers like Dr. James David Manning want to make their audience and followers believe that they are the light of the world, that they will enlighten all Mandinka people, when on the other hand, he and most of the others fall right into that category of a Mandingo slave that fits perfectly to the ideas of the slave masters. Ok so he didn't like the Obamas, so what, but did he have to put them down the way he did on the internet with that squeaky homo voice that was so annoying? He was truly one of the most disgusting Mandingos in the entire population of the United States of America. And as we all know far too many clerics are gay and play on innocent young men in the church.

For me Dr. Manning was just another typical chicken eating preacher that hated himself and all Black people who didn't believe the same garbage that he himself believed. This was and is typical Mandingo behaviour that the White man just loves, for we are now pitted against ourselves. I thought that he bought his Dr. title, because I could not believe for the likes of me, that a man that is suppose to be so intelligent was still in 2011, implementing the White mans techniques and strategies to keep niggers under control by any means necessary. But he was not alone, there are enough large and small fry Mandingos chicken eating preachers out there just like him to fill the void to keep the ball rolling and follow his lead right into hell. You know, I can deal with these small fry Mandingo Niggers that try to put their brothers and sisters down by posting BS on the internet, but when it comes to degenerates like the Honourable Pastor James David Manning, this is where I have to draw the line. I would never be associated with a back stabbing "DEPENDENT" Mandingo like him. And he was suppose to be a man of God? What he was, was the devils advocate in person and the perpetrator of evil. Any Black person that has the opportunity to help turn around some the hatred that we have for ourselves should in my opinion be doing just that, instead of driving the nail deeper. But I'm sorry to say that he was never alone, there are thousands of chicken eating preachers just like him out there just waiting for the chance to say something negative about themselves and their race. He was an ambassador of the devil and just as bad as all the other Black males and females that try to put the African American Mandinka people down and doing this all in the name of the Lord to help keep his brother subdued.

But why did he lie on God? You and I know very well that God did not tell him to do and say such things about Black men and women; it was the devil and he was his advocate. And if God did he was also referring to Manning as well, because he was disguised as the devil himself, ignorant chicken eating preacher talking loud and saying nothing. Manning missed his opportunity to really do something good for the community, instead he just bad mouthed us all. He should have tried to come up with a solution instead of making things worse, did he not see that he was playing right into the hands of the White devil and delivering his brothers to him at the same time? Sorry but for me, he was one of the most disgusting clerics that I have ever seen. Since when did God say that Black men have no honour??? That a 100% lie on God. Where was his honour? His demeanour and the things that he said about Blacks were definitely not honourable. And all the Mandingos attending his services and church were just as much to blame as he was because they listened to that BS, and maybe that is why he had to leave early.

Personally I think that there is today an overload of clerics which are homosexual in our church-all churches from catholic on down to whatever denomination that you can name. And when a person that is suppose to be a man of God has to trim young boys for their sexual and immoral misconducts and desires is a poor excuse for them to say that they are priests, ministers or bishops. And in the case of Bishop Eddy Long for instance we should really stop and think about what's going on with these homo preachers; now here is man that has been scrutinized by his fellow bishops ministers, peers and the news media. And of course any man that wears a wig when he's preaching his sermon cannot be serious about the Gospel word and truth. In America homosexuality is very, very prevalent in all dominations, especially Black churches. And people of the New Birth church in Atlanta, now you see what is happening and how you have been "bambooseled" out of your Tides, because Long was, according to the interviews, screwing boys in hotels, condos and even the church. Now we all know that he's going to hell for that.

Eddy long manipulated those young men for his personal satisfaction without any shame and or reverence for the Lord. And the only thing that reverend Long could say in his defence was "I never portrayed myself as a perfect man" (sound like Clinton) don't it? This of course means to me that he is admitting that the allegations are true, and contrary to popular belief, you can't solve this problem with prayer; it goes deeper than that and the allegations were so strong against him, that all he could do was to pay up and shut up. I'm sorry people but the Gospel word is not for sale. And in the words of Pastor Tony Smith I would like to share this quote with you. "What has happen to people that we would allow anybody with any type of conversation to come in and seduce us in the church when we have the Bible" by this he meant that everything you need to know is in the bible, and that no chicken eating preacher should come in and tell you anything different. The main downer about the internet is that there are far too many ignorant Mandingos online talking all kinds crap about sisters; and another figure out

The Internet

there on the scene but not professing to a man of God is SpeakDaReal. I must say that on the one hand, that Speak DaReal has some interesting things to say-for instance when he spoke about the Black adolescent pregnancy rate. "What was the mother of that girl doing to allow her 16 year old daughter to get pregnant"? Where was the mother? Did the boy stay over night there? Or was she just one of them little whores running the street?

On the other hand SpeakDareal has the same mentality as the late Dr. Manning, which is to try and put Black people down especially Black women… And this really pi…s me off because SpeakDareal is actually racist against Black women, and any "Biach" that is married to a White Woman, and has nerve enough to talk about his mother, sister and daughter the way he does, is no better that those Mandingos in West Africa who are dismembering and murdering their people on a daily basis-and that's what he is doing; the exact same thing, only with words and if he was born in West Africa he would be one of those Mandingo henchmen. Yeah you speak da real alright-da real BS, with that half yellow little nigger on your webpage, and just like that Mandingo BS that you possess, you will teach him to do the same as you…But on the other hand there are young Black men out there like JAYLOVE 47 who seem to have his head in the right place, but there are far too few of them.

But in general SpeakDareal is just as much against Black women as many of the "Internet Coons" that try and put the Black woman down. Black man you are no better than your sister, as a matter of fact you are worse because she is not telling the world how lazy your Black AZ really is, don't want to work, and expect someone else to enable you and your laziness. And all of the things that she is saying about you does not even come close to that what many Mandingos are telling the world about sisters, and it's time for you to wake up- either you s… or get off the pot, turn in your nigger card, and find a way that you can turned yourself lily white, because that is what you really want to be. That is why this book is called" I know why Mandingos sing", because far too many internet Coons out there are always singing like a jail bird telling the world just how stupid you really are. The point is that Mandingos forget too easily; and all you young punks out there and some old ones too have forgotten what the White man has done to you and is still doing it-these atrocities I can never forget.

Black men you should unite not against Black women but unite yourselves against the things that the White man has done and is still doing to you. All of the things that he has done throughout the many years to keep you under control, the job market, housing, unfair prison sentences in comparison to Whites for the same crime etc. and all you punk Mandingos out there who still have that Mandingo mindset are still helping the White man to keep you under control. But I have a question for all you punk Mandingos out there on the internet who are talking all this BS about sisters, which is "How Do You Want Her To Be"? She has already been everything to you, but as soon as she start demanding that you get yourself together, you start talking crap, so what do you want? Because the only thing that people are hearing from you is mouth. Black men have blown this thing so much out of proportion that shows like "Reality Rehab" are using the phrase "Angry Black Women" to drive traffic to their website, and not to mention the word "nigger", they got Europeans and Asians calling each other nigger now days. One of the major problem with Black men in America is that they do not know who they are; because if they did they wouldn't be saying the crap that they are saying about Black women, and like Steve Harvey said "older Black men have missed the opportunity to teach our young Black men the principles of manhood" and he's 100 % right. I've said this before and I will say it again, Black women are the epitome of womanhood, (the White man knew that back then) and as I have said, there is absolutely no mention of a White woman in the Holy Scriptures. So Mandingo straighten up and earn some respect for yourself, because you know it's a sad day when Mandingos get on the internet want to make a comment about something somebody said, and the first thing that they do is to roll up a splif.

Here are some of the stupid things that Mandingos are saying that I pulled off the internet to let you see just how crazy and stupid some Mandingos have become in their quest to discredit Black women and themselves. Here one Mandingo wrote...

"RECRUITING AND TRAINING EAGER TO LEARN (SMALL TOWN) WHITE GIRLS FOR THE BLACK MEN'S MOVEMENT." "WE'VE PRETTY MUCH HAD TO GIVE UP ON BLACK AMERICAN WOMEN AS THEY WERE TRYING TO CIRCUMVENT OUR CAUSE BY FORMING A MILITARY-STYLE COUP D'ETAT TO OVERTHROW THE BLACK MAN'S AUTHORITY AND LEADERSHIP WITHIN THE MOVEMENT -- MUCH LIKE THEY'VE DONE WITHIN BLACK HOMES ALL ACROSS AMERICA!"

Now this is a really stupid Mandingo here; and the only direction that Black men like him are going to move is deeper into the clutches of the White woman. There is NO movement, there is NO Coup d'etat, and the only movement that these type Mandingos are involved in is moving towards Becky. Is this guy really saying that he is declaring war on the Black woman? Is he saying that he is ready to take up arms against his mother, sister and daughter that he left her mother for to be with a Becky? Is he saying to us that his little Black daughter has to stand by and watch him degrade Black women? If that is the case then the only thing that I can say is Lord help us because niggers done sho-nuff gone Becky blind because it's really sad to read such BS and to see just how much the internet is helping in the demise of Black people especially the Black man; and here he is the Black man, with the help of the internet is helping the White man to accomplish his evil and destructive goals. But remember, this is that destructive nature of Mandingo.

You see that all over Africa, North America, South America and the West Indies as well. But most Mandingos are too stupid, and are not interested in knowing where the real problem lies so they try to put the blame on the Black woman because she had to exert some type of authority over them so that the White man would not kill their black AZ. You see that's that Hutu against Tutsi Mandingo crap that we saw in Sierra Leone, West Africa.

The **Sierra Leone Civil War** began on 23 March 1991 when the Revolutionary United Front (RUF), with support from the special forces of Charles Taylor's National Patriotic Front of Liberia (NPFL), intervened in Sierra Leone in an attempt to overthrow the Momoh government sparking a gruesome 11-year civil war that enveloped the country and left hundreds of thousands dead and homeless.

Exodus out of Freetown... West Africans flee their land and homes with little more than the clothes on their backs-the RUF joined with the AFRC to capture Freetown with very little resistance from Blood diamond rebels who were found guilty of murder, rape and mutilation. I'm sure that some of you saw the footage, and the things that were going on in Sierra Leone, the way those people were dismembered, because they were taller, or they voted for the wrong party, is a poor as hell excuse for niggers to act like that; they severed peoples legs, cut of their hands and ears, and as we all know and have seen, some Mandingos take it to the extreme-whether in America or in Africa, Mandingos are the same all over the world.

Chapter XII
The Conclusion

Africans have a long standing tradition which dictates that others shall provide for them. The children are suppose to take care of the parents, and this type mentality has of course spilled into the mix in America. Just as our African counterparts we expect the government and anybody else that we can talk out of their money, time, goods or whatever to support us. Every time you turn around "Negras" are expecting you to bring them this, loan me that. Just like our counterparts in West Africa do it. The truth of the matter is that all African American men, women and children are descendents of the descendents of a brutal and decedent people.

Hate to say it but, just like our ancestors we have that inner hatred for each other, rather than for our captors. But Black people don't think that you have nothing to offer society because that is just a lie. A lie that you have been believing since the White man learned that he could exploit and kill you whenever he wanted to. Just remember Black Africans were the builders and rulers of Ancient Egypt and the surrounding territories such as Sudan; and Black Nubia have the most number of Pyramids of all, app. 250.

White people have never had Pharaoh or Emperors or Dynasties. There aren't any White people on earth that can claim such amazing achievements as the Nubia who are the ancient creators of the Pyramids, and up until today scientists are still trying to figure out how they designed them. Black Africans were the Pharaoh, kings and queens. The only thing that White people can claim as far as ancient history is concerned is that they also come from Africa themselves. The first person to

124

assume the title *Rex Anglorum* (King of the English) was Offa of Mercia, 757 and he ruled until his death in July 796. Africans have had kings and queens long before whites came out of their caves. Ramses II ruled Egypt from 1279 BC - 1213 BC. He ruled for 66 years, and in that time had several wives, 48-50 sons, 40-53 daughters and was the first Pharaoh of the 19th Dynasty. He was also Pharaoh during the time of the Jewish Exodus from Egypt, led by Moses. The 1st ruler of what has been called Egypt was Asar, who the ancient Greeks called Osiris. He was the leader of the "Nubian" colonist that colonized what is now called Egypt. Asar was deified as a God upon his death and became part of the worlds 1st known Holy Trinity which was comprised of Asar, Aset and Heru, who the ancient Greeks called Osiris, Isis and Horus. And according to the bible the first Pharaoh of Egypt was Shishak also known as Pharaoh Shoshenq l. He ruled from 944 to 924 B.C.. So Black people we have so much history that it is unbelievable.

You know, it took me a long time to come to write the words which you have been mentally consuming and as a rule I don't usually talk about Black problems in this manner especially where Caucasian people can read my thoughts; but since I ain't ruling nothing I'll go on and speak my mind; and after long consideration I decided to try and relate to you exactly how I feel about the controversy between African American women and African American men relationships.

As we all know Black men are still being tarred and feathered, ripped apart by horses, and whipped to near death; but today it's the media, police brutality, and segregation in the job market. Police brutality against Americans in general is at an all time high especially when it comes to Blacks. But the killing part is, Black cops are sometimes more brutal to Black males than White cops are; but in general, this is just another form of the "Tar and Feather" act. Even though we have Mandingos in the highest positions that you can have in

America they seem to still be afraid to speak up for the African American cause, they are letting the chance slip by them. Back in the day the White man used the radio to keep Whites informed as to the where about's and what the niggers were doing, but they don't have to do that today because the Black man is keeping him very informed about what he is doing and his current family situation.

Mandinka living in America in 2011 are suppose to be the modern Mandingos, but we have not changed one bit since the 13th century; we still mirror that which our ancestors did to each other since many of us converted to Islam, and our relationships to each other have gotten worse. The things that we do and say about each other, and how we still kill each other have escalated to an all time high and getting worst by the day. This at least helps me explain the situation a little more, we have it, we can't deny it, but we don't recognize it. You see, my reaction is only the result of me realizing what has been done to me, where I come from, and what diabolical means were created especially to keep me under control, and anyone that has any kind of sense at all would be p...ed off. I do not hate White people, have many White friends-but I am smart enough to know and realize what has happen to me and do something about it, because "I am the master of my faith, I am the captain of my soul". But the big question is, how do we turn this all around, how do you turn around something that has been taking place for decades? It won't be easy, but it's not impossible.

Brothers and Sisters we all know the story because this has been going on for hundreds of years and you already know what the White man has done to us. So now what are we going to do about it? Are we going to continue to demoralize each other to the point where the Mandinkan people in America have destroyed all sense of reality? And the White man is just sitting back laughing at his well trained niggers. I think that we have to start at ground level in order to straighten this mess out.

Mandingos and Mandingorettes alike have to take the time to teach their young Mandingo male and female offspring at an early age their worth. They don't know their worth, especially the males. You have to realize that Mandingos are easily hurt, and they go into submission, you can't talk down to your children, you can spank their little buts if they are not obedient, but you can't whip them, Mandingos then will either submit or become aggressive. And we all know the BS about the fatherless homes and fatherless children.

Black men you have to be that role model which your child desperately need and is seeking. But it will probably be put on the Black woman's shoulders because they have had to in the past keep everything together; but I hope that will not be the case. But in order for this to happen, Black men have to get that African do nothing, sit under the Baobab tree and let your woman take care of you, deceiving, blood thirsty attitude and mentality out of our heads, because this is why the situation among Black men and Black women in America is escalating; too lazy to work, trying to be that slick Mandingo nigger.

In order to break the cycle we all as Black parents have to teach our children the "Real African American History" in order to help them get out of the cycle. We are not responsible that we were born as Mandinka, but we sure can do something to curb the animosity and killings. What is there to be jealous of? We all possess the same basic intelligence, and have the same chances. The white man has already given them to us, but most African American don't take advantage of them. Other groups like Asians can come to America and become successful, but Mandingos don't seem to get it. Why? Because of our "lazy by nature ways", wanting to be comfortable but not having to exert any energy doing it, (the Baobab tree syndrome). The African American Mandinka woman has to do the same, but I must say that she is more industrious than Mandingo. But too many of them are laying around having baby after baby and relying way too heavily on the social welfare system to take care of them and their kids (the African American Female Mandinka Syndrome).

Black Mothers

Sorry but I don't understand the teen pregnancy rate Black mothers? The question for me is, what are you doing or not doing to allow your 14, 15 or 16 year old daughter to get pregnant at such an alarming rate? Don't you have things under control? This is not an accusation but a question. Give your daughter the possibility to make the right decisions in life. Express the need for an education, and stop laying on her back all the time…

Black mothers, you have to take on a new mind set and transfer it to your daughters and sons as well and stop having so many babies, especially if you have a daughter. If she sees that her mother has 4 kids form 4 different men, then she will more than likely do the same thing because this is what she is accustomed to. It's a shame and shocking to know that Black women and girls in America have a 72% adolescent out of wedlock pregnancy rate, which makes them the #1 whores in America-don't get me wrong now, White girls will screw at the drop of a hat, but the adolescent out of wedlock pregnancy rate is the lowest in America.

It goes back to that female Mandinkan way of thinking; you have to express the need to get an education or some type of documentation of achievements; if it is not possible to get a college education, then try learning a trade. Blue collar workers sometimes earn very good salaries. Or a career in the military- and speaking of the military, I really can't understand why Blacks hardly ever consider joining the military, you don't have to make a career out of it, but Uncle Sam will definitely give you an education. And while you are getting your education Uncle

Sam will also pay you a monthly salary, feed you and put a roof over your head. And if you are smart and can't afford to go to college, then the military is the way to go, all you have to do is give Sam a little of your time and you got it. But if they have nothing, they will not be able to survive in our society, now days it's about education, and education is the significance of life. With an education one can move mountains, but if they don't have at lease a high school education, even the military will not accept them.

I know that pier pressure is high on children and sometimes it's hard to keep control, but if you can in any way possible don't allow your child to only speak Ebonics, make sure that their English skills are good first and never allow Ebonics in your house. What they do outside the home is another thing, and you can hardly control this, but when they are home please don't speak or allow your child to speak this ghetto Ebonics BS. It's just being lazy and in my opinion this is one of the things that are helping to keep our young Black male and females down.

As I said it's a thing of laziness, and Mandingos are good at this, but what they don't realize is that it is just as easy to do it right as it is to do it wrong. Instead they speak and write this stupid form of English and it's hurting them, they don't realize it but it truly is. Ebonics is the lazy mans way to communicate in speech and in writing and believe me if you don't think that it affects your English skills then check out what others are saying about Ebonics-because Ebonics will definitely be confuse with the real English.

Here are some quotes that I took from the internet about what some people are saying about Ebonics. These are perfect examples to show how Ebonics will destroy your English. Even though some of the people making comments contend that they speak perfect English, they are still making grave grammatical mistakes. So check them out...

"Ibonics is identity for an african american. like varnacular, ibonics is spoken by those who choose to speak it. One problem though is that most of them (quite annoyingly i think) use it when trying to write formalenglish, they cant distinguish. not trying to praise nigerian's but i reallydoubt one seeing nigerians using broken english in formal situations. however i dont think ibonics should affect nigerians in anyway. its veryannoying when i see nigerians trying to speak ibonics, then even confusing it with proper english. wow. if its a problem for some (i must copy nigerians), i think u should go check your mouth. Lol" "haa, i feel you on this one. "we was eating, what was u saying?"

"It happened to me in my english 101 class. My first essay was a disaster. The teacher was like "Most computercorrect mistakes, yours didn't correct you, and u didn't even see 'em". I typed with word-pad, so yeah u should know i wasn't corrected. I had to control myself from typing stupidly. I talk like that sometimes, u know whenu trying to pull the "shaniqua" look. lol, But i've tried not to let it affect my school work. I think u can do it too. When im studying/writing essays, i kind of go into another "world?"Then again, if that's how you TALK all the time, i don't think it'll be easy for you. No one is perfect, but i think if we try hard, we can be close to being a little perfect. School works are no jokes, exp when u have a wicked teacher. "Beside, u made on mistake spelling "does". Lol"

"hey, i don't kow if any one has this problem too, well i speak english fluently, ofcourse, but i also speak ibonics with some of my friend. (Ebonics is the popular african american way of talking). but i have come to realize that its becoming to affect my english writing skills. For example, if i wanted to write "we were dancing". i would write "we was dancing" and this happens to me in my english papers and essay. but i think i catch my mistake most of the time. so those any one have any advice for me or opinion or even share this same problem"

Mind you, these statements are exactly as I took them from the internet, nothing altered. And even though some of these people think that their English is o.k., it is totally crewed up. But in reality by speaking and writing in this manner, no Black or White person or company will ever hire you for any position except cleaning their toilets. So wise up my young Mandingos; association brings on assimilation. If they grow up speaking and writing like this, it will take hold one day and they will be 99 years old, and will never be able to get rid of it.

I know that many women have to raise their sons alone but I think that shouldn't be a hindrance to how your son will be when he becomes a man, sure there is no man in the house but, ladies that's no excuse-a little secret from a man. If you want your son to act and treat women the way you expect him to then you will have to teach this to him-all women whether there is a man in the house or not have it in their power to mole their sons the way they want them to be-but you can't start when he's 9 or 10 years old, he's too old then, you have to start when he's about 3 or 4 years old.

The woman is always with the child, but not the man simply because he has to work, (that is if he has a job) and is not home at least 50% of the time. So mothers, start when your child is 3 years old to shape and mole him into the man that you want him to be, it's in your hands; don't un-necessarily beat him, the White man did that enough-don't forget he's a Mandingo and he breaks easily, and the next thing you know you have a little monster on your hands. Children today are very smart and they learn quickly, but you have to teach them correctly. Make sure that you instil in him the need to be responsible and give him a since of belonging, make sure to encourage him to always try to do better. You have to build up his confidence at an early age and teach him to respect YOU, and if you do this he will also respect women as well.

When raising boys you have to have a strong hand. My mother was a small woman but she packed a wallop, but at the same time she gave her sons that sense of responsibility that we needed to survive in the White mans world. My dad worked so my mom taught all of her sons, 7 of them to cook, clean, wash and be responsible. So single mothers you have to have a strong hand hand because if you don't they will later become uncontrollable. I don't have to tell you to love your boys, because you have proven this many, many times and many times over.

But tell your sons to keep his pipi in his pants, to start thinking with more than one head, and stop running around the neighbourhood impregnating young girls. You have to express to him the need to change and get some type of education to earn a decent living, not sell dope on the corner to young Black kids and to get out from under the atrocities that were done to the Black man and his "Image" during times of slavery.

So if the female adolescent pregnancy rate is 72% then what is the males? Also 72 percent? No probably much higher; I would say almost double because the way Mandingos are, if a girl gets pregnant from her young lover, he probably got her girlfriend, and 2 or 3 others pregnant as well. Which would make Mandingo the Mega Whores of America. This means that the Black man in America today is living out his ancestral behavior patterns, it's just that we are now in 2011. I know that there are a lot of influences that children are accessible to, and I think that the Black woman and women in general have it in their power to control and mole a young mans personality and character the way she wishes it to be; don't forget 90% of the time women raise men, and if you want your little man to become the man that you think he should be when he grows up, then you as a mother have to take measures that will practically insure that at least he will respect you. If you are a single mom, you have to raise your child with as little drama as possible. If you have a male child don't be changing your male friends all the time-this is especially bad for boys, and if you are not careful 40% of the time your man will screw your daughter and son as well which means that they both would be in danger. I noticed that Black men and women often talk down to their children-curse and make them feel insecure and worthless and this is a terrible way to treat your child; if the child is smart, you see this as a provocation because you were or not smart, and that turns into jealously towards your child, eventually causing that child in many cases to be less mentally active. Still this is that Mandingo mentality which is coming into play, I don't have anything, so why should you-I don't know anything so why should you. And forget about what the law say about punishing your children; now I'm not for abusing kids but if they need it then you better do it because the moment something happens the police will be the first ones who will come and take him away, so think about what is happening to our children and do something about it. Obviously White people don't know this and that is why we have so many mass murderers, because White people haven't learn yet how to control themselves. When a Black man is angry they say that he is an angry Black man, but when a White man is angry they say that he is expressing his opinion. Most Whites don't spank their kids, but you have the largest amount of serial killers among White men than you do Black men; history shows you this and White people are and always have been mass murderers.

Black daughters

First of all I would like to repeat myself and say that Black women just like Black men don't know their worth. Most African Americans don't know that we are the descendents of kings and queens-Blacks built and ruled ancient Egypt. But the White man has constantly driven it into our heads that we are not worth anything more than dirt. When on the other hand they are constantly trying to get what Blacks and other nations have; it's a conspiracy, been that way for hundreds of years, that is why they sent their missionaries to all parts of the world. They would suppress the people kill them and steal their natural resources,

133

such as gold, silver, wood, iron ore, steel, copper and anything that the White man could get their hands on and cheat the inhabitants out of that which was rightfully theirs. Africa is a perfect example, especially South Africa, where there are so many diamonds that you can't shake a stick at em; but who has control? The white man. So my young beautiful Black girls don't think that you are not worth anything, because you are, you have something that no White woman on this planet can compete with. But you have to go with dignity, you have to in other words, get your s..t together... I know that Black women are generally more industrious than men but sisters still have a long way to go as well.

Krishnamurti an Indian philosopher said "education is the significance of life" and he was right, but you cannot depend only on education to give you understanding. Understanding comes through self knowledge, know thy self-this also includes your history. If you don't know your history, you will not know and understand your future. "Education is the significance of life", get an education and documentation-this doesn't mean that you have to go to college; would be better, but the most important thing is to have some type of paper or certificate that says that you have completed and learned some type of skill.

Black women could start by stop having all these babies that you can't take care of, start concentrating on an education, and stop concentrating on screwing. Get yourself a decent education, no matter what it is, any type of documentation that you can get. If you have documents stating for instance that you have completed a training course in toiletry and were looking for a job in this field you would be a more likely candidate for the job than someone who has no documentation at all. But the question for me is, are young Black women not ashamed to know that they have the highest juvenile pregnancy rate in America?? As I said, the Black community boast an amazing 72 % rate in unwed adolescent mothers which is higher than all other groups in

America combined. Surely our overly sex saturated culture plays a large part in this, because teen sex is communicated almost as an expected rite of passage without any consequences, and this a very dangerous message for young people who don't mind taking a chance anyway. And while this recent upward trend is certainly dismaying, it would also be silly to describe it as an absence of education or any other single factor for that matter. Fact remains that something has to be done. It's up to you to do it and of course young Black women have to take on a completely new mindset as well, otherwise it won't work.

And since Black women discovered the social welfare system in America, it seems to be an excuse to get pregnant and let the government take care of them and their children. I know that it's a new day now, but let's face it, White people do have a lot to do with that. But it would seem that in 2011 the need to be successful in life would have increased, but unfortunately this is not the case. And one of the most disturbing things for me to see is young Black women fighting in the streets like cats and dogs; they obviously don't know how this look. But hey, ghetto girls... For me it all boils down to one thing and that is parental guidance, and because of that Mandingo mentality we tend to let things go... The Lord will make a way. Keep thinking like that. If Black parents are not teaching their children to be responsible then how are things going to change for Black people in general? They won't. Sisters it's like this... If you have a decent education you won't have to be dealing with no "good for nothing" Mandingo; you have choices in life and it's your responsibility to make the right choice whether red, yellow, black or white. And some have even gone as far to say that many of the problems with Black women are that they try to keep a man by having many babies for them... That might be true, but only partly true because you still have that Mandingo mentality that is also driving these young women to have babies like they are in a contest. And lets face it girls, many of you do this, but if their mothers had taught them better, many Black teens wouldn't be in the shape that they are in today. Don't forget that the average African woman's life is centered around having baby, after baby, after baby not because she wants to keep her man but because this is what she does. That's her mentality; it's embedded in our culture, and that's almost all West African Mandinka and most all Mandinka men and women living in the western hemisphere.

Black Fathers

One of the most natural things is for a man to protect is woman and family if he has one. Some Mandinka don't do a very good job at this-and don't start trying to blame the White man. Sure they did bad things to us during slavery, but we are partly to blame for that. If our ancestors had not betrayed us, and I'm still glad they did because if they hadn't all African Americans would still be in the bush, and there never would have been slavery in America. Because if Mandingo had that protective instinct, he would not have allowed his woman to go out into the wilderness among lions and tigers and all sorts of wild and dangerous animals to look for food like roots and other edibles. But Mandingo was more than likely scared himself... So he sends his woman out 10 miles from home to fetch the fire wood while he sits on his favourite stool under his favourite Baobab tree.

When the slave masters beat you into submission the Black woman was always there for you and she always will be. But it's a new day now, and it's time for Mandingos to step up to the plate and start taking responsibility for their actions. Obviously you don't care about your own race, and that is exactly why we are in the shape that we are in today. Mandingos have always betrayed each other for personal gain, and I think that all Black men who are referring to sisters in the manner that many do, are leaning a bit far out of the window. I don't think that they know what they are doing. This type of none participating behaviour is being funnelled down to the young Mandingo men in the community, they mirror that which their fathers and older Mandingos are doing, if he beats his wife, then chances are the boy will probably wind up slapping his pregnant girlfriend or his wife around. Many Black fathers are not interested in helping their son or daughter to get an education, and if the child is smart he tells him that he will never amount to anything anyway. And by doing this they are preparing the child for a life of uncertain actions and deeds and many problems that could have otherwise been easily avoided if the father was a more hands-on dad; but instead many Black fathers talk down to and are sometimes menacing to their children.

Ghetto gang fights and killings have become a daily occurrence; weapons, narcotics, you name it, is all the result of this negative Mandingo way of thinking. And we all know that an apple does not fall far from the tree. It holds to truth that if you as a parent are not motivated then your child will also not be motivated unless it's to steal, sell narcotics or kill each other. And I do think that there are enough Black male roll models around to get the job done, and I thank God that my dad was a hands on dad, he gave us freedom but you couldn't get away with everything-my mom on the other hand was different, she would lock your jaws in a heart beat, that is if she could catch you...

Black dads, you have to instil in your sons the need for them to get an education and not rely on the streets to provide for them. Sure it's easy money, but they are also helping the White man to keep us down, because nine times out of ten White men are usually in cahoots with Black drug dealers and as a result are bringing large amounts of drugs in the Black and other communities; and don't say that Mandingo is doing this because he has no job, he's not looking for one especially when it is easier for him to make money on the street, he thinks... Because this practice is deadly and one day he will get killed because of that Mandingo mentality which is all around him, and before you know it you have a drug deal that has gone bad, because he was taken out by one of his own whose only purpose was to rob, kill him and take his drugs and money. I know that not all but most Black parents want to give their child the best, but the best gift that you can give your child is to be a hands-on parent. Baba, you have to be a father to your son and not his buddy, there is a big difference here because it's impossible to be a good and proper parent if you are your kids best friend, kids need good and intelligent parental guidance. How can you tell your best friend that he can't stay out until 3 in the morning even though he's only 15 years old-this does not work, and any child psychologist will tell you this.

Teach your son to respect not only Black but all women, and stop calling them "bitch", this alone shows disrespect, but many girls now days except that, and as Don Curry said, "women use to get angry when someone would call them a "bitch" but now days if you call a woman a "bitch" she's trying to figure out where she know you from". But most of the time he is this way because you dad, don't respect his mother and other women, and naturally me mirrors that what you do. Black men I hope that you know that we are the last dogs on the Totem Pole-that's right. Starting from White on down to whatever colour that you want to name, other races, even poor bastards like the untouchables in India, think that they are better than you; that's how bad our reputation has gotten Black men, but as I said before I cannot put all races in the mix because, many Greeks and Turks and Italians (old country that is) hold Black men high in esteem. But in general our reputation is shot; sure we enjoy respects in fields such as sports or music, but Black man you have to do something. Back in the 60s people had more respect for Black men in America because we would fight-but you punks now days are just pu....s and only kill each other. And speaking of Black male pussies, yes that's what I said; anytime that a man has to take out his frustration on the woman which he calls his mate, his lover, his all in all, beat her and damage her mind and body, is for me a p...y-men that attack women will hardly ever do the same to a man whether Black or White. Reason being is that he is not always 100% sure that he will not get the s... kick out of him, that's why.

Black Sons

You know, boys are sometime difficult to control, but they learn at a very early age who to mess with and not to. But Black fathers, even if they are not in the household have to start at some point to teach their sons how to survive in life without having to rely on illegal activities to earn a living. And why is it that many ghetto kids believe that their lifespan will only be between 19-21 years? Because of the Black-on-Black violence; sure one could connect this trend to Black males, but Black gangster sisters are all over the place as well. And as I said before, we are victims of our own mental and spiritual start of mind. We brought this killer mentality with us from Africa, and 300 years later it has not changed. When you look at the turmoil which smother many African people, 90% of the time it is in West Africa whence we come. It means nothing now days for young Black men to kill each other; it's not only about drugs and territory, it goes deeper, much deeper, and some of them Mandingo niggers out there actually video tape the killing and their victims, how stupid...

But young Black men, there is absolutely no reason why you should put Black women down the way you do. You first of all are no better, but you blast it all over the internet and on videos about your dislike for African American women. One reason is that you, like all lazy Mandingos don't want to step up to the plate; they get these girls pregnant, and if and when they finally ask them for money to help support the child that they help cerate, they say that Sapphire is a gold digger, but you will help pay for that White woman's child that you didn't even father.

The White man has always said that all you wanted to do was to screw his sister, and as I have already said, for many Black men this is very true, for others on the other hand it's not because for many Black men the only thing that a White woman can do for them is to tell them where a Black woman is. But if you have to get yourself a Becky I wish you well, but don't give up on who you are just for her. Because it's a total turn off for me when I see Black men betraying their own mothers, sisters and daughters with one of those 300 pound bouncing Becky baby girls the way that many of them do. But many Black fathers have a lot to do with this trend, because they themselves are mostly uneducated and have no interest or intent in trying to better his or his sons position in life in any way at all.

But there is one thing that I have to give these watered down Mandingos credit for which has to do with our music and that is the fact that young Black men today have taken Black music production and distribution and put it in their own hands, especially for Hip Hop music, keeping 100% of the profits for themselves and not having to give 95 % of it to the White man or the Jew. Other than that, most of these watered down young Mandingos are total disasters, and for all you young guys out there, YOU have to break the cycle. You have to start at one point in your life to do it different. You have it in your hands to build and raise the reputation of Black men to the highest. So will the real Mandingo please SIT DOWN! Because the rest of you Mandingos out there are standing up for the wrong reason.

It has already been proven that Blacks are the inventors of many of the everyday things that we use in our everyday life-we are not dumb or stupid, just lazy. And Black people especially

Black men have to get away from this stigma. Worthless, lazy, dumb, good for nothing, are all adjectives that you hear describing the Black man. And believe me, it doesn't stop at Black men because Black women are jut as lazy; you see this type behaviour in the way many Black women have to rely on the welfare system to survive and keep their families alive and going in this country.

Some people even try to contend that Rap or Hip-Hop music is partly responsible for the present dilemma of our youth today. I contend that Rap music has nothing to do with it at all; but many Black people are under the assumption that many of the problems of our youth have much to do with Rap and Hip Hop music. This is the biggest Mandingo bull that I have ever heard. 2PAC is DEAD and so is BIGGY SMALLS. And all you Mandingos running around here in America should really get this out of your heads, because many of them are still living in the past, still want to be the best dealer on the block, still want to have the best RAP. And I see many older Black men running around looking like they are just coming from a HIP HOP concert around the block, but my question is; how can a 45 year old man dress and walk around looking like his 12 year old son, with baggy pants on, still be straight in the head, and think that someone is going to respect him??

Rap music is only one result of the Mandingo mentality-and as I have already mentioned before, the Mandinka people were and still are their own ENEMY. And that is what is so prevalent in our people and community today; and that is why we kill each other and not blink an eye, that is why we sit around all day and wait for someone else to help us, this is why our young daughters have baby, after baby until the percentage rate for unwed mothers in America has risen up over 70% of the population. That is why many of our women are on social welfare, that is why our men cat around impregnating as many women as they can, that is why we are not responsible, that is why we niggers beg, that is why we are easily influenced to do the wrong thing, that is why we shoot each other in the head, that is why we have the highest HIV infection rate in America, that is why Black women act the way they do, that is why we have chicken eating preachers, but most of all that is why 2PAC is dead.

That is why we make the best music, that is why many young whites want to copy our live style, that is why Black men are lazy, that is why Mandingo love Becky, that is why Sapphire loves Bobby, that is why we speak Ebonics, that is why we are the best dancers, that is why White women want Black men, that is why Black women are angry, that is why we are so entertaining, that is why we don't like each other, that is why Whites stay in the sun, that is why White women get butt and lips implants, they want to look like Black women as much as they can, they want that sister girl butt, they want that sister girl body and they want that sister girl look. And it all boils down to one thing; betrayal, betrayal that started way back in the 13th century. But you can never tell me that White people don't envy us, what we have, and what they stole from us but they will never admit this. This is a fact and Black people still don't know their worth, especially Black women.

But on the other hand, what would White people and the world do without Black people and other minorities? Nothing... First if there were no Black people Portuguese and Arabians would not have had the possibility to enslave them, Jews would not have gotten rich, we would not have High Life music, you wouldn't have anybody to be jealous of, you wouldn't have anybody to call nigger, wouldn't have anybody to hang, wouldn't have anybody to whip to death-unless you beat yourself, your women wouldn't have to pad their a...s, because there would be no competition. Wouldn't have to sit in the sun all day trying to get our colour because all of you would be pale face, you would always win in sports because you would only be playing against yourself, never would have had slavery and you would have had to pick your own damn cotton. Sports would not be exciting, and all of your music would sound like classical, German Schlage, Country or Hillbilly music. We wouldn't have traffic lights, wouldn't have hip hop music, or blood banks. You wouldn't be able to rape our women. There would be no Dr. Defreeze, wouldn't have rock music, would not have had Rag music, no Dixie. Wouldn't have jazz music, wouldn't have refrigerators and there would never have been Elvis.

Believe me, I am not trying to explain to you the behaviour of the Black man or Black woman in America, I'm only trying to explain it to myself; we, meaning all of us are playing out our natural instincts to be envious, deceitful and distrusting to each other, which is exactly that what the slave owners used against us to help keep us in bandage. But the $64.000 question is-what are we going to do about it and where are we going from here? Because not all African American males think and act this way, the idiots that share this mind set are usually from the ghetto or some place similar, have no formal education, usually fathers that are missing and just good for nothing and DEPENDENT on Becky. You can see this in many of the videos that are being put up on Youtube and Media Takeout etc.-stupid not thought out videos which are actually giving you nothing but the opinions of stupid Black men who are usually drugged out or sitting on their bed trying to conduct a video conversation with a 40 in his hand. These guys are helping the White man keep control over Black men and Black women in America-the slave owners didn't want the Negro male or the Negro female to operate as a family unit because he knew that it was dangerous for his survival. And I think that if we do not repair and turn around the roles, the Black family structure will eventually completely collapse in America. Many Black men leave their families because of that Mandingo West African mentality that was brought to the United States of America by our forefathers; they don't know it but believe me that is why; and if you are a descendent from West African Mandinka people, then you are endowed with this Mandingo mentality that was given to us by our ancestors. But the point is that we are in the "New World" now and we have to rid ourselves of the brutal way of thinking and acting which is our inheritance, and help our youth become better citizens and human beings.

Earlier on in this book I mentioned and named many Black athletes and musicians who conquered that white stereotypical, attitude against Black males and females and if they can do it so can you. In doing so, we will raise a generation of young African-Americans that will truly value marriage, family and self. Today Blacks have more chances to make something out of themselves than they ever had, and if whites can send a man to the moon using only 10% of their brain, then we as Mandinka can surely get together and use our minds to conquer our problems. And if a tiny five foot tall African Mandinka woman could organize such a massive and long lasting protest against the Jewish and White establishment, and become the leader of the most controversial political and humane movement in African American and American history, which was the Underground Railroad then maybe we all should rethink our worth.

Black people have always blamed White people for our dilemma, sure they helped enslave us, but it doesn't stop there. Once African Americans recognize the West African Syndrome, that the Jew and White man has for so long played upon, we can then start to conquer it. Eliminate the idea that the White man is keeping us down and start to do something positive with your life, then we as African Americans can hold our heads up high. We have to instil in our young people that, it's not all about drugs, not about where you come from or what colors you wear. Obviously most of our young people today are only concerned with that ghetto type mentality; you hear it in the music and see it in the way they dress and dance. If you want to know where you are going then you have to know where you come from. What I'm trying to do is to get Blacks to see a pattern; a pattern that Black men and women follow all the time which makes us our own enemies and prisoners of that Mandingo mentality, and we kill each other not because of economical or even religious reasons we do it because that is what we have learned, it's in our genes and it is what we do. We must teach our boys and girls their God-given roles at an early age. We must teach our boys how to become men who think creatively, and learn how to solve problems without the use of violence. We must teach them how to become "mentally strong for it far outweighs being physically wrong". We must teach them how to be independent and how to be gentlemen starting at a young age. We must teach our girls how to choose a strong man with good character and values and be independent and trustworthy with sound values and goals.

Of course we all know that drugs and narcotics are helping to keep many Blacks down and under control, but it has gotten so bad that most couldn't quit even if they wanted to. All sorts of uppers and downers and designer drugs have been placed in the Black communities for one purpose, and that is to keep the Mandingos under control and to cause tribal warfare among our people.

So Black people we all have something to offer society, and if you think otherwise then you are just fooling yourself and believing the lie that you have been hearing every singe day since the onslaught of slavery when the White man learned that he could kill and exploit you anytime he wanted to. Just never forget that Black Africans, were the builders and rulers of Ancient Egypt that's all you need to know, to know how brilliant Black people really are.

There aren't any White people on earth that can claim such achievements; the Nubia are the Ancient creators and architects of the Pyramids, and Black Africans were the Pharaoh's kings and queens. And there is not much that White people can claim as far as ancient history is concerned because White people just don't have such a rich historical past as Blacks.

Black Achievements

But it doesn't stop here, oh no... Here are some reasons why I say that Blacks don't know their worth. Let's face it, there are many things in the American culture that all Americans hold dear to heart even though these things were invented by Blacks, but White America still perceive us as second class citizens. Things that ordinary citizens like you and me take for granted every day. Now I don't know what you think, but all these invention are detrimental contributions to a decedent White society who's only purpose is to destroy the Black image.

Here Are Some Bright Moments in African American History:

THOMAS L. JENNINGS (1791–1856)

Was an African American tradesman and abolitionist. He was a free black who operated a dry-cleaning business in New York City, N. Y. and was the first African American to be granted a patent. Jennings' skills along with a patent granted by the state in New York on March 3, 1821 for a dry cleaning process called "dry scouring" enabled him to build his business. And he spent his early earnings on legal fees to purchase his family out of slavery.

146

BLOOD BANK - Dr. Charles Richard Drew (1904-1950)
The idea of a blood bank was pioneered by Dr. Charles Richard Drew (1904-1950). Dr. Drew was an American medical doctor and surgeon who started the idea of a blood bank and a system for the long term preservation of blood plasma. His ideas revolutionized the medical profession and saved many lives and we know the rest of the story.

BLOOD PLASMA - Charles Richard Drew
Dr. Charles Richard Drew was an American medical doctor and surgeon who started the idea of a blood bank and a new
system for the long-term preservation of blood plasma (he found that Plasma kept longer than whole blood). His ideas revolutionized the medical profession and have saved many, many lives.

GAS MASK - Garrett Morgan-(1877 – 1963)
The gas mask was invented by Garrett Morgan, an African American inventor. Morgan used his gas mask to rescue miners who were trapped underground in a noxious mine. Soon after, Morgan was asked to produce gas masks for the US Army.

TRAFFIC SIGNAL Garrett Augustus Morgan-(1877 - 1963),
Garrett Augustus Morgan was an African-American inventor and businessman. He was the first person to patent a traffic signal. He also developed the gas mask and many other inventions.

THE REAL McCOY - Elijah McCOY, (1843 -1929)
Elijah McCoy was a mechanical engineer and inventor. McCoy's high-quality industrial inventions (especially his steam engine lubricator) were the basis for the expression "The Real McCoy," meaning the real, authentic, or high-quality thing.

LEWIS H. LATIMER. (1848-1928 Light bulb)
Lewis Howard Latimer was an African-American inventor who was a member of Thomas Edison's research team, which was called "Edison's Pioneers." Lewis Latimer improved the newly-invented incandescent light bulb by inventing a carbon filament

(which he patented in 1881).

MADAME C. J. WALKER, (1867- 1919)

Madame C. J. Walker was an inventor, businesswoman and self-made millionaire. Sarah Breedlove McWilliams C. J. Walker was an African-American woman who developed many beauty and hair care products that were extremely popular with her cosmetics business. Her first product was a scalp treatment that used petrolatum and sulphur.

THE POTATO CHIP

The potato chip was invented in 1853 by George Crum. Crum was a Indio /African American chef at the Moon Lake Lodge resort in Saratoga Springs, in New York. French fries were popular at the –George Crum restaurant and one day a diner complained that the fries were too thick. Although Crum made a thinner batch, the customer was still unsatisfied. Crum finally made fries that were too thin to eat with a fork, hoping to annoy the extremely fussy customer. The customer, surprisingly enough was very happy - and thus the potato chip was born.

PEANUT BUTTER – George Washington Carver (1865?-1943)

George Washington Carver was an American scientist, educator, humanitarian, and former slave. Carver developed hundreds of products from peanuts, sweet potatoes, pecans, and soybeans; his discoveries greatly improved the agricultural output and the health of Southern farmers. Before this, the only main crop in the South was cotton. The products that Carver invented included a rubber substitute, adhesives, foodstuffs, dyes, pigments, and many other products.

SUGAR PROCESSING - Norbert Rillieux (1806-1894)

Norbert Rillieux was an African-American inventor and engineer who invented a device that revolutionized sugar processing. His multiple effect vacuum sugar evaporator made the processing of sugar more efficient, faster, and much safer. The resulting sugar was so superior that his apparatus was eventually adopted by sugar processing plants all around the world. There are untold, government patents for inventions that can be attributed to African Americans-the Drop Mail box, Dyes for the sides and soles of shoes, a machine for embossing (contouring the paper) of photographs, leak stopper for hoses, The Folding Bed and many more were all invented by African Mandinka Americans.

But isn't it ironic that the musical instrument that our forefathers used to communicate with each other with, was also used in the capture of our brothers and sisters; that same instrument and also the most primitive, and yet so modern to suggest that it could be evil; was the DRUM, and how many peoples or nations can you name that were able to create a system of communication based on rhythmical patterns which could be sent, heard and understood over miles at a time?

The African Black man hardly had a chance because they hit them from all sides, a 100% conspiracy against the African people and that what they possessed. There were enormous profits to be made at each and every stage of the North Atlantic sugar, rum, gun, economic and financial slave transactions and in the process, Europe and America became rich while Africa bled to death. But the discovery of America in 1492 changed the picture because it transformed what was up until then a small trade in ivory, gold and slaves into an intricate global network of trade, piracy, scoundrels and politics, and in the process, the political landscape of most of Europe went through successive transformations from feudal to an industrial setting, paving the way for colonialism in the 19th century.

The slave trade was not a business for the common man. Since it required enormous capital, it remained the privilege of emperors, noblemen, and other scoundrels with money. Portugal of course wanted to keep it's monopoly on this trade and sought justification of its position because of their early discoveries. But the lure of huge profits was too great to keep out interlopers. French and English pirates were active against Portuguese shipping throughout the 16th century. Rich European merchants in London, Liverpool, Paris, and Amsterdam financed the expeditions, and on occasions, even their monarchs participated. And in both Spain and Portugal, it was the kings who had titles to the trade monopolies.

To simplify the complex interplay between the Muslims, Christian Europe and Africa, we can divide the slave trade into several periods. The first period started with the Portuguese capture of slaves in southern Morocco (1441) and ended with the discovery of America in 1492. The second period lasted until 1541, when the Sultan of Morocco recaptured the powerful fort of Santa Cruz and drove the Portuguese from it's Atlantic coast line.

Another in 1578-1640 was marked by Dutch superiority in the Atlantic and the Indian Oceans, and between 1640-1713, there was a bitter struggle between the Dutch, French and the Brits for control of the slave trade routes; which ended with British control and superiority.

After these crusades the Dutch were basically broke and many of their holdings on the coast of Africa and in the Indian Ocean had fallen pray to many of their enemies. England established itself on the southern coast of Guinea in West Africa and the nations of Ghana and Nigeria, while the French won control over the northern coastal lines of Senegal and Gambia. And in that same year, the British and the French won concessions from Spain to supply slaves to the Spanish colonies in America. The last period 1713 to 1818 saw the Atlantic slave trade in full bloom and the systematic transfer of millions of West African men women and children to the Americas and broke down many African social structures.

White people have always wanted what Blacks have, you see that in the way they systematically take everything from you, our gold and diamonds, land everything, even God. And that is why he portrays Jesus and the Disciples in HIS likeness, because

150

as I have already said, it is jealously and greed for what the Black man possess (including his woman) and that is why he tries to hide the Black presence in the Bible, especially Black women. But he feels that he cannot have relations with the Oedipus, which means that he cannot have sex with the likeness of the mother of Jesus which was NOT a White woman, who he has now made White... Pure. Thus creating sort of a dual Oedipus, because he wishes to have relationships with his mother, but society forbid this; but there is the maid or mammy, so he can act out his childhood fantasies now that he has become a man, and act this out without any social consequences, because the mother is now Black, thus not in the image of the White Virgin Mary. Black people problems today have little to do with White people because our problems go much deeper than mere White people, because if that was the case we probably could have easily gotten rid of this curse by now. We've had these problems long before Europe even started to exist, and there were Black kings and queens when White people were still crawling around in the darkness of their caves in Europe.

When I was a kid in school in the south, we had to use the hand me down books that were given to our school by the Whites schools; this handicapped Black kids very much because we were not up to date, and this helped to keep the Black children's educational level down. Today as we all know Black kids are not learning anything because their parents don't know or not teaching them anything-the teachers in the schools can only teach them so much but we as parents have it in our hands to shape and mole the child into a decent responsible individual. This would obviously be a Mammoth undertaking, because there are just too many Mandingos who really don't care about the situation at all. Guys that will kill you as soon as to look at you. What we need to do is to increase public awareness of the sadistic epidemic of Black-on-Black crime, and create general educational and media awareness, through print, radio, billboards, and on-line forums; teach our young people that they have VALUE, and to give them a little insight into what we have achieved throughout the many centuries; if there were no Black people there would be no White people.

Basketball players, football players, musicians, artists, golfers, politicians; our national heroes have it in their power to help turn around many of the problems, but it has to be on a national level, they can do commercials for instance to help motivate young Black males, because many of our young Black men are not motivated to do anything, unless it has something to do with violence or selling narcotics, and we have to take this urge away from them by embracing our history for what it really is and teach our young, that they come from a people that has a history that Whites can only dream about. I know that many Blacks in America advocate that we should forget all about the atrocities that the Jewish and White slave masters did to us, but such things should never be forgotten, we have to keep score- this is the only way to keep our sanity and keep alive who we are, and just as the Jewish people will never ever forget what the Germans did to them during the Holocaust we should never ever forget what Jewish merchants did to us and what happen during the brutal and purposely sustained North Atlantic slave trade.

"I Know Why Mandingos Sing" points out many things about the West African Mandinka people, our psychological makeup and the North Atlantic Slave Trade that many blacks as well as whites are unaware of. It represents years of research, study, gathering material, information and interviews, and is presented to you as a documented account of and comparison to the psyche of the West African and the African American Mandinka people. Provocative-historical accounts of the West African Mandinka secrets and attitudes that have kept us down since the 13th century. In search for the true meaning and an explanation behind the true mentality of the African American mandinka people, (what makes them do what they do) I have probed and searched extensively, for an answer from the Rock of Gibraltar to North Africa to Europe and back to America.

You were taken all the way back to the 13th century to help me explain my theory about the psyche of the West African Mandinka people and how it compares to modern day Mandingos living in America today and bring to the forefront, and discard the notion that Jews, Whites or any other race of people are responsible for our overall psychological makeup, and that African Americans are no different from their counterparts living in West Africa. There have been many books written about the impacts of slavery on the African American negro, but this is the first time to my knowledge that anyone attempts to explain and address the "origin" of the problems that African Americans have with each other and are confronted with on a daily basis. I hope that this book will get some people thinking and shine a new light on the many problems and attitudes concerning all African Americans today; and to my knowledge, there has not been any material written or published about the "true" psyche of the Mandinka people; this book hits Black America in the heart, and gets down to the "nitty gritty" of explaining why African Americans act the way they do. Carefully constructed with chronologically illustrated pictures, the book is also aimed at communicating to young Black youth their worth by showing them only a few of the many accomplishments that great Black men and women have contributed to society, and that Blacks in America have contributed just as much to American society as Whites have and more than any other ethnic group in the United Stated of America. "I Know Why Mandingos Sing" is also about the mental and physical attitudes and deeds that make African Americans so venomous towards each other, and that Black people have a great history to be proud of. Sometimes humorous and informally written this book focuses on many of the aspects seldom discussed concerning the North Atlantic

Slave Trade and the development of the Mandinka people throughout the last 148 years. This book is not for everyone, there is a special audience that I am trying to reach in this account.

This book is not about African Americans or Africans singing, it's about the un-justice that has been bestowed upon Blacks in America by Jewish and White slave owners with their Mandinka helpers on their side, in their bid to capture and destroy their brothers and sisters. "I Know Why Mandingos Sing" is also about the psychological structure and non-caring attitudes that make African Americans kill each other the way we do, and an attempt to answer the question of where the Black-on-Black violence comes from and find out *"The Real Reason Why Blacks In America Are So Deadly To Each Other.*

I Know Why Mandingos Sing...

Many of the traditions of African American Mandinka encompass many different cultures and represent a Black lifestyle in America that is unprecedented in many western countries. Mandinka in America are "loosing face" and the only thing that will help and save us is a radical evaluation of our values as human beings and as a people. Our youth is dying out at a rapid pace and this pleases the White man because he contends that there is a surplus of niggers anyway.

I know why Mandingos sing was written to bring about the awareness of our inheritance as a brutal and deceitful people. This photo illustrated account of the path that untold Mandinka people had to take and endure are only reminders of the terrible injustices and atrocities that were bestowed upon us by the hands of unscrupulous Jewish and White slave merchants.

Many West African Nations have already lost their membership card to humanity, and the African Americans are well on their way to accomplishing the same thing, because the African American Black man is slowly loosing respect as a decent human being all over the world; the Black mans reputation, as far as the White man was and is concerned has never been worth a hoot, and now it has dwindled down to practically nothing, and this is practically due to the fact that Blacks kill each other for apparently no reason at all.

Oh yes, Whites love Black music, the Black athletes that keep sports alive and the Black musicians that keep the world dancing, but fact remains that Mandingos in general have a bad rep, and that goes for Black males and females alike-so in his quest to discover the truth Don has maybe hit upon some of the answers... But the question is, what are we going to do about this enormous problem of Black and Black-on-Black violence that we all face in the African American community on a daily basis?? I know why Mandingos sing is a must read for every African American, and it was written for every Black person living in America, all the mothers, fathers, sons, daughters, aunts, sisters and brothers, and traces the terrible path that untold Mandinkan people had to take and endure; and is a reminders of the terrible injustices and atrocities that were bestowed upon then. The book gives you a stunning and detailed picture and account of the development of the African American community since slavery, and the psyche of the modern African American Mandingo as compared to that of West Africans today.

About the Author

Don is Founder CEO - RCMG-3 Marketing Group, Development and Product Manager- is a Web developer and innovator with many ties in the international community. Don attended Sacramento State University in California where he studied Music/Art and Business Administration. Don is also the recipient of the *2003-2004 National Leadership Award*, "**Honorary Chairman**" *of the Business Advisory Council, presented by **The National Republican Congressional Committee USA**.*

He has completed many courses in business management, direct customer one on one sales, and is also winner of the prestigious International Web Masters and Designers "**Golden Web Award** " 2003-2004 for his design of the Website known as "**Rates-and-Tariffs.com**"; he became interested in computers and computer design, and honed his skills as a web designer/ developer and innovator over a period of twelve years. His specialties are Website Design, Affiliate/MLM Marketing and search engine Optimization *(SEO)* Services.

Don is very committed to helping steer beginning marketers, entrepreneurs and start-up business owners in the right direction to help enhance the experience and profitability of their online business. RCMG/WEMP-Solutions is now committed to helping young Blacks in America through the internet and have opened up their Affiliate marketing school especially to help young Black males and females get a better start in life. It's free and anyone can join us, all you have to do is register at http://www.rcmg-3.com.

I Know Why Mandingos Sing...

CreateSpace Direct
Bookstores and Online Retailers
Web: http://www.iknowwhymandingossing.com
Title ID: 3692969
I SBN-13: 978-1466355866

10 9 8 7 6 5 4 3 2 1
First Edition, first printing: November 2011
Printed in the United States Of America